AUSTRALIAN NATIONAL MARITIME MUSEUM

Published by Hordern House
for the Australian National Maritime Museum.

Printed on Raleigh Tomohawk Text
and finished in May 1996.

The edition is limited to 950 copies.

Nine hundred copies are hand bound in quarter midnight blue
Scottish calf with marbled papered sides
designed by Margo Snape.

A deluxe issue is limited to 50 copies,
numbered and signed by Dr Kevin Fewster,
hand bound in full midnight blue calf
and presented in a custom made solander case
bound in taupe Oxford Library Buckram.

Printed and hand bound in Australia.

John Thomas Seton, *Portrait of Alexander Dalrymple,* oil on canvas,
915 x 710 mm, 1765. Private Collection, United Kingdom.

This is the only known portrait of Dalrymple as a young man and was most
probably painted for his eldest brother, Sir David Dalrymple of Newhailes, after
Dalrymple's return from India in 1765. In a pose characteristic of the Edinburgh
portraitist Seton, the sitter is portrayed with all the accoutrements of his position of
East India Company ship captain, including a Blaeu globe, a map and chart, and a
pair of dividers.

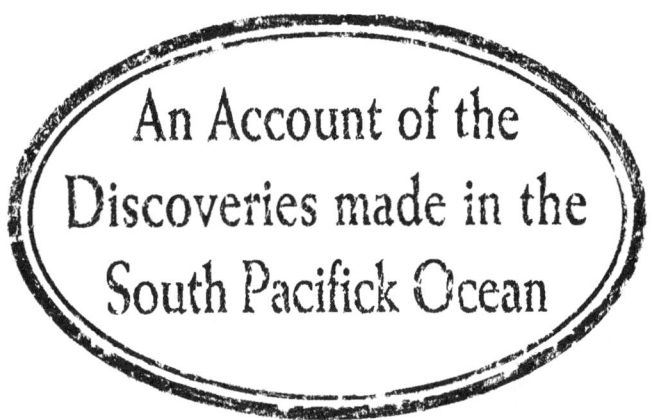

An Account of the Discoveries made in the South Pacifick Ocean

by
Alexander Dalrymple

First printed in 1767,
reissued with a foreword by
Dr Kevin Fewster of the
Australian National Maritime Museum
and an essay by
Dr Andrew Cook of the British Library

HORDERN
HOUSE

Hordern House
77 Victoria Street
Potts Point
Sydney 2011
Australia

Australian National Maritime Museum
Darling Harbour
Sydney 2000
Australia

First published in 1996 by Hordern House Rare Books Pty. Ltd.
for the Australian National Maritime Museum

Edited by Kathryn Lamberton
Printed in Australia by Southbank Book
Hand bound in Australia by Newbold & Collins

National Library of Australia
Cataloguing-in-Publication Data

Dalrymple, Alexander, 1737-1808.
An account of the discoveries made in the South Pacifick Ocean previous
to 1764.

Bibliography.
ISBN 1 875567 13 5.
ISBN 1 875567 15 1 (deluxe ed.).

1. Australia - Discovery and exploration. 2. Polynesia -
Description and travel. I. Cook, Andrew S. II. Fewster,
Kevin. III. Title. (Series : Australian maritime series ;
no. 3).

919

ISSN 1037-1338.

FOREWORD

With the launch and recent voyages around Australia of a replica of James Cook's ship, *Endeavour,* it seemed only appropriate that the third title in the Australian Maritime Series should be linked to Cook's great voyage of discovery 1768-71 during which he explored Australia's east coast and claimed this territory for Britain. Neither the book reissued here, nor its author Alexander Dalrymple, are well known to Australians. However, as you will see, Dalrymple's writings were of great importance in shaping the climate in which Cook undertook his epic voyage of discovery.

For each of the first two books in this series, an expert from the Museum's staff wrote the introductory essay. On this occasion, we have invited Dr Andrew Cook, Map Archivist of India Office Records at the British Library, London, to contribute the scholarly essay. Dr Cook is widely acknowledged as the world's leading authority on Alexander Dalrymple, having written his doctoral thesis for the University of St Andrews after nearly twenty years research into Dalrymple and his publications. (Dr Cook is not related to Captain James Cook.)

History usually remembers the great achievers and discoverers. Dalrymple never saw Australia; indeed, the thesis he proposes in this book is that the Australian land mass would prove to be only an outlier of the much discussed Great South Land. Why, then, is the book important to Australia's history?

Dalrymple was hopeful that he might be appointed to take a Royal Navy ship into the Pacific to observe the transit of Venus in 1769 and then on to seek out the supposed Great South Land. As Dr Cook shows, *An Account of the Discoveries made in the South Pacifick Ocean previous to 1764*, was written and printed by Dalrymple to advance his claims for this command. The book was officially first published in 1769. In the book, Dalrymple speculates on the existence of a 'great southern continent' to balance the land mass of the northern hemisphere. Given the state of knowledge of the day, it was a reasonable hypothesis which could only be disproved by systematic, physical exploration. His proposition regarding a Great South Land was duly refuted by Cook's first two great Pacific voyages. But had Dalrymple not been so forceful an advocate, Cook might not have been asked to test his theory. Through its extensive research, Dalrymple's book provided Cook's expedition with the most complete navigational analysis available at the time for the region.

An Account of the Discoveries made in the South Pacifick Ocean... was also of direct importance to Cook during his *Endeavour* voyage as the book contained Dalrymple's representation of the Spanish explorer Luis

Vaez de Torres' course in 1606 through Torres Strait separating Australia and New Guinea. Dalrymple had given a copy of the book to Joseph Banks and mention of it appears in Cook's journal. It is tantalising to speculate how much its contents might have influenced Cook's course towards and up the east coast of Australia.

It is one of the ironies of history that had events panned out differently Dalrymple might have been on board *Endeavour,* possibly even in command. The primary public objective of *Endeavour*'s voyage was to take observers to Tahiti to witness the rare astronomical occurrence of the transit of Venus across the sun, but secret Admiralty instructions also required Cook to seek out the supposed 'great southern continent'. When the Royal Society in London late in 1767 addressed the matter of who should be chosen to undertake this observation, Dalrymple emerged as their favoured choice. He was described as 'having a particular Turn for Discoveries, and being an able Navigator, and well skilled in Observation'.[1] Dr Cook shows that Dalrymple's then recently issued book, *An Account of the Discoveries made in the South Pacifick Ocean...,* had been aimed precisely at securing this end. But Dalrymple insisted he would accept the appointment only if he were given command of the ship. The Royal Society duly submitted his name and terms to the Admiralty where the matter apparently rested for some months. Dalrymple later claimed he had even played a hand in recommending the *Earl of Pembroke* (renamed *Endeavour*) as the appropriate ship for the voyage. While there is no corroborating evidence to support his assertion, the sequence of events leading to the ship's selection and purchase do suggest that, contrary to popular belief, the *Earl of Pembroke* was chosen before Cook was considered for its command and that Dalrymple had input into the vessel's selection.

On 3 April 1768 the Royal Society's President reported to his Council that the Lords of the Admiralty had rejected Dalrymple's nomination as 'such appointment was totally repugnant to the rules of the navy'.[2] The Admiralty's insistence that its ship be under the command of a naval officer was not a matter for negotiation, however a recent article by the eminent Joseph Banks' scholar, Harold B. Carter, points out that seventy years earlier the Admiralty had readily appointed a Fellow of the Royal Society, Edmond Halley, to command a Royal Navy ship on three scientific voyages into the Atlantic sponsored by the Royal Society.[3] True to his word, Dalrymple declined to accept the appointment as observer with someone else as voyage captain for, as he later wrote, 'a divided command was incompatible with the public service in such voyages'.[4]

While Dalrymple might have been disappointed, no one could deny that Lieutenant James Cook was superbly qualified to lead the voyage. After joining the Royal Navy in 1755, Cook had displayed remarkable talent as a navigator and cartographer, and furthermore, in 1766 had observed an eclipse of the sun. History subsequently honours Cook as perhaps the world's greatest ever navigator and ocean explorer.

Dalrymple, by comparison, is scarcely remembered, although his cartographic contribution to eighteenth century knowledge was outstanding. True to the aim of our Australian Maritime Series, it is hoped that the publishing in facsimile form of this rare work, together with Andrew Cook's scholarly essay, will better establish Alexander Dalrymple's rightful place in Australian maritime history.

Kevin Fewster
Director
Australian National Maritime Museum

[1] 'Minutes of the Council of the Royal Society of London', vol. 5, 17 November 1767, in H. T. Fry, *Alexander Dalrymple (1737-1808) and the Expansion of British Trade,* London, 1970, p. 117.

[2] 'Notes written by Joseph Banks of transactions at the Royal Society, 3 April 1768', J. C. Beaglehole (ed.), *The Journals of James Cook: the Voyage of the Endeavour 1768-71,* Cambridge, 1955, Appendix II, p. 513.

[3] H. B. Carter, 'The Royal Society and the Voyage of HMS *Endeavour* 1768-71', *Notes and Records of the Royal Society of London* 49, 1995, pp. 246, 252.

[4] 'Memoirs of Alexander Dalrymple, Esq.', *The European Magazine and London Review* 42, 1802, p. *325.

CONTENTS

Followed by

An Account of the Discoveries made in the South Pacifick
Ocean previous to 1764

A C K N O W L E D G M E N T S

The Australian National Maritime Museum and

Hordern House Rare Books Pty. Ltd.

gratefully acknowledge the generous sponsorship of

Sevist Pty. Ltd.

which has made available the

rare original from which

this facsimile edition has been made.

ALEXANDER DALRYMPLE:

Research, Writing and Publication of the *Account*

•

Andrew S. Cook

When Alexander Dalrymple, an East India Company servant based at Madras, returned to England from Canton in July 1765, it was not with the idea of offering himself as leader of an expedition to observe the transit of Venus in the South Pacific Ocean in 1769, nor with the expectation of setting the British agenda for southern hemisphere exploration for the rest of the eighteenth century. His mission was more mundane. It was to propose to the Court of Directors of the East India Company in London that they should establish a commercial settlement at Balambangan, north of Borneo, to take advantage of the China and south-east Asia trade. Yet within three years, Dalrymple had issued the first findings of his research into the routes of Spanish and Dutch explorers from Mendaña to Roggeveen, had redrawn Robert de Vaugondy's map of the South Pacific Ocean, had refined the scientific arguments for the existence of a 'great southern continent', had proposed himself (through Adam Smith) to Lord Shelburne, Secretary of State for Colonies, and to the Earl of Chatham to lead the next discovery expedition after Wallis and Carteret, and had been nominated by the Royal Society (at the recommendation of the Astronomer Royal, Nevil Maskelyne) to lead their Transit of Venus expedition to as yet undiscovered islands in the South Pacific. He was then thirty years of age.

The Early Years

Dalrymple was born in Scotland on 24 July 1737, the eleventh child of Sir James Dalrymple, second Baronet, of Hailes, in the county of Haddington, and Christian Hamilton, youngest daughter of Thomas, sixth Earl of Haddington.[1] There was a family tradition of professional competence and public position: Sir James had followed his father as Member of Parliament for Haddington Burghs and as Auditor to the Exchequer of Scotland. Alexander's childhood was spent at the family home of Newhailes, near Edinburgh, and at school at Haddington. When his father died in 1751, he was nominated, through family connections, to a writership in the East India Company. Though under age, he was appointed in November 1752 and arrived at Madras in May 1753. As a writer Dalrymple worked in the Secretary's office and, with the influence of George Pigot, Governor of Madras, as Clerk to the Committee of Accounts under Robert Orme, later the Company's historiographer. Orme allowed Dalrymple to use his private library and, as Sub-Secretary from 1757, he combed old Company records in Madras for references to expeditions and trade in Cochin-China, Borneo and the Sulu Islands.[2]

In 1759 Dalrymple's career diverged sharply from the pattern of East India Company service in Madras. He declined the position of Secretary, and instead persuaded Pigot to authorise an experimental trading voyage to the Philippines, Borneo and Sulu, where he obtained a grant of land for a Company settlement at Balambangan. In 1763 he proposed to return to London to explain his plan, but wintered in Manila and left Canton only in January 1765.[3]

In the autumn of 1765 he returned home to Scotland after a thirteen-year absence.[4] Newhailes was in the possession of his eldest brother David, who had married in 1763, and his mother and his two sisters were living at home. It was almost certainly then, rather than on any later visit, that the Edinburgh artist John Seton was commissioned to paint the portrait of Alexander Dalrymple which appears as the frontispiece to this edition.

Dalrymple's Research Begins

In London again, Dalrymple joined the Pigot household in Soho Square, and turned to his geographical collections. He later said that 'from the time he returned to England in 1765, [he] was almost constantly engaged in collecting and arranging materials for a full exposition of the importance of the Eastern Islands and South Seas'. His collecting had begun when he acquired some Spanish histories of the Philippines during the French siege of Madras in January 1759, and he dated his 'first collection of South Sea Voyages' to that time.[5] During his own voyages Dalrymple had collected books and manuscript charts, plans and navigation accounts, particularly from Spanish sources. In London he focused on the early Spanish and Dutch voyages in the Pacific, in search of the last undiscovered continent.

The Pacific Ocean was the least known part of the world in 1765. The coastlines of America and Asia had long been defined on maps, but the islands of south-east Asia – Borneo, Java, Celebes, Moluccas and Philippines – marked the eastern limit of confident knowledge. The north and west coasts of Australia had been outlined by the Dutch from the *Duyfken* in the Gulf of Carpentaria to the *Leeuwin* on the south-west coast, but between Tasmania and New Guinea nothing was known. The archipelago to the east of New Guinea was a continuing mystery, and the geographical relationships of Pacific island chains south of the Equator equally uncertain. The ocean from the west coast of New Zealand to Easter Island, in many places as far north as 20° South, was commonly left blank, giving scope to theories of a 'great southern continent'.[6]

Though discoveries were made on Spanish and Portuguese voyages in the half-century after Magellan,[7] the first westward voyage of intentional South Pacific exploration was that of Alvaro de Mendaña in 1567 to Santa Isabel and San Cristobal in the Solomon Islands.[8] Mendaña's attempt to return on a colonising expedition with Pedro Fernandez de Quiros in 1595 brought his ships mistakenly to the Marquesas, and then to Santa Cruz, where Mendaña died.[9] Quiros led a further expedition in 1605, with Luis Vaez de Torres, landing first at Henderson Island, then skirting east of the Tuamotu Archipelago and north of the Cook Islands, before arriving at Espiritu Santo in the New Hebrides.[10] The ships were there separated by the weather, Quiros returning to America and Torres continuing westward along the south coast of New Guinea, to discover and thread the strait which bears his name, on his way to Manila.[11]

The Dutch voyage of Jacob Le Maire and Willem Schouten from Juan Fernandez in 1616 passed through the north of the Tuamotu Archipelago, and the northern Tonga Islands, to Horne Islands, and then negotiated New Ireland, New Hanover and Admiralty Islands in the Bismarck Archipelago, before coasting the north side of New Guinea.[12]

In 1643 Tasman's expedition from Batavia passed south of the known west coast of Australia, discovering the southern coast of Tasmania and the western coast of New Zealand. His voyage continued through the Tonga and Fiji island groups to Ontong Java and New Ireland. He entered the Bismarck Sea at the west of New Hanover, and coasted the north of New Britain and New Guinea considering it to be continuous land without the through passage he expected to the Arafura Sea.[13]

Jacob Roggeveen's first object on leaving Juan Fernandez in 1722 was to locate land reported by Edward Davis in 1687 as lying in 27° South, '500 leagues' west of Chile, but the discovery he made in that latitude was Easter Island, further to the west. From there he passed through the north-west of the Tuamotu Archipelago, the western fringe of the Society Islands, and the Samoa Group, before making land at New Ireland.[14]

All the trans-Pacific voyages kept, or were driven by wind and current, to tropical latitudes for the ocean crossing, and consequently all after Mendaña passed through islands now identified as the Tuamotu Archipelago. None found the larger islands of Tahiti, Fiji or Samoa, but all treated their western Pacific landfall (even Quiros' Espiritu Santo) as part of a mainland, to be skirted for safety. None except Tasman, and possibly Roggeveen, made significant inroads into the 'great southern continent', Tasman confining the eastward extent of Australia and giving a westward limit (the west coast of New Zealand) to the supposed continent. The long east-west distances travelled by dead reckoning, with indeterminate currents, made the assessment of reciprocal longitudes problematical and the geography of the islands east of New Guinea difficult to map.

Dalrymple had no such modern knowledge. He had some form of early published narrative for each of these voyages:[15] Herrera for Mendaña's first voyage;[16] de Morga's publication of a letter from Quiros, supplemented by Thevenot's fragment of Figueroa, for Mendaña's second voyage;[17] Torquemada and two of Quiros' memorials for Quiros' and Torres' voyage.[18] For Le Maire and Schouten he used near-contemporary parallel Dutch accounts;[19] he relied on Valentijn for Tasman's voyage;[20] and he was aware of the differences between the Dutch and French editions of Roggeveen.[21] He was less concerned with the voyages of William Dampier and Willem de Vlamingh, who arrived in Australian waters from the west. Dalrymple respected the approach of de Brosses' *Histoire des navigations,* with its geographical table of voyages advancing the case for systematic exploration in the South Pacific and Robert de Vaugondy's compilation maps of the Pacific Ocean and 'Australasie' attempting to reconcile the different narratives.[22] This collection helped him to assess the significance of his discovery in 1765, at a London bookseller, of two composite volumes from the library of the seventeenth-century French minister Colbert.[23] One of these volumes included a printed memorial of the 1630s sent by Juan Luis Arias to Philip III of Spain, incidentally summarising the routes followed by the 1606 expedition, particularly of Torres on the south coast of New Guinea after the separation.[24] Torres' own relation of his voyage had fallen into obscurity in Spanish archives,[25] leaving on maps only a tradition, without clear authority, of the separateness of New Guinea from land to the south.[26] Dalrymple had seen, among papers in Madras, only a map of Torres' discoveries on the south coast of New Guinea,[27] and the Arias memorial confirmed for him Torres' track from the New Hebrides to Manila, as well as clarifying some of the obscurities of Torquemada's account of the early part of Quiros' voyage. Dalrymple translated long extracts from the Spanish, Dutch and French narratives,[28] and first published his translations in two quarto volumes as *An Historical Collection of the Several Voyages and Discoveries in the South Pacific Ocean,* the Spanish voyages in the first volume in 1769/70 and the Dutch voyages in the second volume in

1771.[29] He freely acknowledged de Brosses' *Histoire des navigations* as his model, and borrowed directly de Brosses' table of discoveries with their published or manuscript sources.[30]

Dalrymple's *Account*

The present work, *An Account of the Several Voyages and Discoveries made in the South Pacifick Ocean previous to 1764,* was written by Dalrymple in 1767 from the same body of information as later generated the two-volume *Historical Collection.* The *Account* is in three sections, the first and longest, 'A Geographical Description of Places', comprising descriptions, from the published voyages, of landfalls, sightings of land, and observations of phenomena taken as indicative of the proximity of land, all entered on the map engraved to accompany the text. In the second section, 'An Examination of the Conduct of the Discoverers in the Tracks they pursued', Dalrymple analyses, so far as possible, the intentions and decisions of each expedition leader at crucial points in the narratives. Defining the purpose of the *Account* as being to lead to 'a Southern Continent' (p. xix), he restricted its scope to the ocean 'between America and Papua on the South of the Equator' (p. xvi).[31] Dalrymple's third section, 'Investigations of what may be further expected', represents the fullest exposition of the counterpoise theory in the argument for the existence of a 'great southern continent' before its effective disproof by James Cook. Here he also summarises the associated theory that the prevalence of certain winds at particular seasons denoted the proximity of land masses. Described as 'Part I', the *Account* represents only part of Dalrymple's early concept of his larger work, and was to be followed in a second part by a chronological series of the texts of the voyage accounts already discussed.

For the 'Chart of the South Pacific Ocean' in particular, Dalrymple reassessed from the voyage narratives the relative positions of the Pacific islands each had seen. The result differed markedly from Robert de Vaugondy's map of the southern oceans in de Brosses,[32] not only in the reciprocal longitudes of South America and Australia as the two outer limits, but also in the distances sailed by each expedition between sightings of land. Dalrymple was here further refining the improvements which Bellin had made in 1742 to Guillaume Delisle's map of the southern hemisphere, in the reciprocal positions of Pacific islands, positions which were then used by Robert de Vaugondy.[33] He allowed Mendaña to have sailed further than Robert de Vaugondy had thought before reaching the Marquesas, and consequently pushed Santa Cruz westwards, closer to its correct position north of the New Hebrides. He reined in the notion of the distance Quiros and Torres had sailed together, and correctly separated Espiritu Santo from the Queensland coast to which Robert de Vaugondy's map had attached it. The consequence (or purpose) of Dalrymple's changes was to emphasise the area between Tasman's New Zealand and the meridian of 90° West as unpenetrated, and to show the various signs of land reported by Juan Fernandez, and by Quiros, Lemaire and Davis between 15° and 30° South, as the northern perimeter of the continent. Dalrymple referred interested readers to the section 'Data, on which the chart of the South-Sea was formed', though this was not present in the *Account:* he may have intended to give it in the proposed second part, but he eventually published it in *Historical Collection* in 1769.[34] In that form it summarises, chiefly from the 'Geographical Description' of the *Account,* the statements Dalrymple used as authorities for calculating the positions of islands on the chart.

The first sign that Dalrymple's *Account* was in preparation came in a letter from Adam Smith to Lord Shelburne in February 1767:

I send you enclosed Quiros's memorial presented to Philip the second after his return from his voyage, translated from the Spanish in which it is published in Purches. The Voyage itself is long, obscure, and difficult to be understood except by those who are particularly acquainted with the geography and navigation of those countries; and upon looking over a great number of Dalrymple's papers I imagined this was what you would like best to see. He is besides just finishing a Geographical account of all the discoveries that have yet been made in the South seas from the west coast of America to Tasmans discoveries. If your Lordship will give him leave he would be glad to read this to you himself and shew you on his map the geographical ascertainment of the situation of each island. I have seen it; it is extremely short; not much longer than this memorial of Quiros. Whether this may be convenient for your Lordship I know not. Whether this continent exists or not may perhaps be uncertain; but supposing it does exist, I am very certain you will never find a man fitter for discovering it, or more determined to hazard everything in order to discover it.[35]

The first suggestion that Dalrymple was considering a publication had come in his letter of 24 November 1766 to the Earl of Chatham as Prime Minister, pressing his claims (from his Eastern Archipelago voyages) to be considered for future expeditions.[36] As a consequence, Shelburne as Secretary of State used Smith's connections with Alexander's brother David to discover more of Dalrymple's activities and plans.

Dalrymple had arrived in England during the revival, after the Treaty of Paris, of government interest in exploration 'to the advancement of trade and navigation'. His name had already come to the Earl of Egmont's notice in the Admiralty in 1763 when Captain Kempenfelt, returning to England with despatches after the capture of Manila, had recommended him as the source of his information on South Pacific exploration. According to Dalrymple, Kempenfelt promised Egmont that he would introduce Dalrymple to him on his return to England but, when Kempenfelt told him that Egmont wished to meet him, Dalrymple declined the introduction out of loyalty to Pigot (then an opponent of Egmont).[37] This may explain Dalrymple's absence from involvement in 1766 in the preparations for the expedition of Samuel Wallis and Philip Carteret to the Pacific.[38] Egmont's secret instructions of August 1766 directed Wallis and Carteret simply to search for the 'great southern continent' in the South Pacific Ocean, between Cape Horn and New Zealand.[39]

The Voyage to Observe the Transit of Venus

It was clear to Dalrymple, on the fringe of the Royal Society in 1766, that the Society's resolution (and the intention of the Astronomer Royal, Nevil Maskelyne) to observe the transit of Venus in southern latitudes on

3 June 1769[40] would prompt another expedition to the South Pacific, to be planned before Wallis and Carteret returned. The phenomenon of the transit of Venus across the face of the Sun occurs four times each 243 years, at the conjunction of the orbits of the Earth and Venus; it is predictable, of only a few hours' duration, and visible only from those parts of the Earth in sunlight at the time of transit. The importance of the transit of Venus to astronomers in the eighteenth century was that, as a unique distant phenomenon visible from different points of the globe, observations of differences in its apparent duration could provide data for calculations of the diameter of the Sun and thence of the Earth's distance from the Sun, the basis of the scalar dimensions of the solar system.[41] The transit had been observed first in 1639, and its recurrences in 1761 and 1769 predicted. Edmund Halley had shown that observations taken in widely spaced latitudes within the 'cone of visibility' would produce the most accurate calculations,[42] and accordingly Nevil Maskelyne went to St Helena for the 25 May 1761 transit.[43] The paper of Thomas Hornsby, Professor of Astronomy at Oxford, to the Royal Society in 1766 drew attention to the 'cone of visibility' for the 3 June 1769 transit which, though widely visible in the northern hemisphere summer, would be seen in the southern hemisphere only in a small area of the Pacific

Ocean. From his own study of the voyages of Mendaña, Torres and Tasman, he drew up a table of seventeen 'suitable' island groups between 4° and 21° South and between 130° and 190° West of Greenwich.[44] For all his proficiency in astronomy, Hornsby had based his analysis of voyages on John Campbell's 1744 edition of John Harris's *Navigantium atque Itinerantium Bibliotheca*, supplemented only by a 1757 French note of Mendaña's Marquesas of 1595. He gave the source of his table of the geographical positions of the Pacific islands as 'Mr. de Lisle's map of the southern hemisphere', i.e. Guillaume Delisle's 'Hemisphere Meridionale' of 1714.[45] All Hornsby's island names and positions were those of the 1714 Delisle map, except that he overrode Delisle's longitude for the Marquesas with a calculation based on Mendaña's old estimate. Hornsby's 'Terra Australis' was simply Delisle's 'Terra Australis de Espiritu Sancto', and all his supposed longitudes had long since been revised by Bellin, Green and Robert de Vaugondy.

Dalrymple was aware that any observers sailing for the 'cone of visibility' of the transit of Venus in the South Pacific would have to discover their own observation station. He very much wished to lead such an expedition, and turned his historical collection of Pacific voyages to serve that ambition. He had attended the Royal Society first in March 1766, was present again on 19 February 1767, and Dr Morton read his communication 'On the Formation of Islands' to the Society on 2 July 1767.[46]

The Royal Society committee 'to consider of the places proper to observe the ensuing transit of Venus; and the methods, the persons fit, and the particulars relative to the same'[47] met on 17 November to hear papers from Maskelyne, John Bevis, James Short and James Ferguson, whose different ideas of destinations reflected continuing uncertainty about the geography of the South Pacific.[48] Maskelyne generalised these uncertainties into the single recommendation of 'such places of the South Seas, as shall be proper for the purpose, and at which they shall find it practicable to establish themselves for making the Observations'. Bevis and Short had named suitable observers in their reports, but only in Bevis' list does Dalrymple's name appear. However, when the committee reported on 19 November, Maskelyne recommended that 'Mr. Dalrymple ... will be a proper person to send to the South Seas, having a particular turn for Discoveries and being an able Navigator and well skilled in Observation'.[49] He was one of five candidates formally invited to attend the council on 18 December for interview,[50] and he replied in an enthusiastic letter to Dr Morton, the Secretary, on 7 December.[51]

It was in this context in 1767 that Dalrymple

'printed a few copies of a tract on *The Discoveries made in the South Pacific Ocean'*. The title-page of the *Account* confirms this, and he noted in the preface dated 1 July 1769 in the quarto *Historical Collection* that he had done this 'above two years ago' when 'motives, which it is unnecessary to lay before the public, induced me to print the tract above mentioned, in a very imperfect state'.[52] Whether or not he was circulating the substance of the *Account* privately in the summer of 1767, it was clearly ready with the chart in or after October 1767[53] for the Royal Society committee and council meetings at which his eligibility was to be assessed. Private circulation of copies of an unpublished book is difficult to track, but it is known that Carteret saw a copy of Dalrymple's *Account* in Batavia early in June 1768.[54]

As a document to advance a personal case, the *Account* is impressive in its tautness, not least because its major part, the geographical description and map, is a cogent distillation from a large body of narrative material. Dalrymple prefaced the narrative with selective autobiographical notes (pp. i-xi), designed to demonstrate his fitness for the expedition. His bibliographical notes on sources, and a chronological table of voyages, occupy much of the remainder of the preface (pp. xxi-xxxi).

The story of Dalrymple's selection by the Royal

Society, the Admiralty's rejection of him for the command of a ship, and James Cook's subsequent commission and appointment as Royal Society observer, has been summarised in the Foreword. But aspects of it have a bearing on Dalrymple's continuing involvement, and his use of the *Account,* in 1768. Dalrymple's stipulation that he would not undertake the expedition unless in command of the vessel was of long standing: he made it quietly plain to Chatham in November 1766, through Adam Smith to Shelburne in February 1767, and to Dr Morton when accepting the Royal Society invitation to interview in December 1767.[55] He was not formally nominated by the Royal Society, as were Dymond and Wales to observe at Hudson's Bay, but simply 'recommended [by the President, the Earl of Morton] to the Lords of the Admiralty for the command of a vessel'.[56] This recommendation was thought to make Dalrymple's appointment sufficient of a formality for him to examine possible ships for the expedition.[57] He was present at the Royal Society council on 3 April 1768 when the Earl of Morton reported that he 'had been informed by their Lordships that such appointment would be entirely repugnant to the regulations of the Navy' and, after attempts at persuasion, he 'persisted in declining the employment of observer, unless he could be vested with the sole command on this occasion'.[58]

He may even have helped modify the crucial minutes: the rough minute book at this point originally read 'entirely contrary to the usage of the Navy' and 'employment of observer for the Society' without a conditional clause following.[59] He continued to be invited to dine at the select Royal Society Club,[60] and only when Wallis returned on 20 May 1768 with news of the discovery of Tahiti, enabling Morton to confirm to the Admiralty on 9 June a destination for *Endeavour,* was there hard evidence to complement the theories in Dalrymple's *Account.*[61] Dalrymple gave Joseph Banks a copy of the *Account* before he left London on 16 August to join *Endeavour* at Plymouth.[62] Later he marked the chart in one copy of the *Account* with the 'Limits where the Transit of Venus is visible from beginning to end' (the 'cone of visibility'), though for whom and why is not precisely known.[63] And, the octavo *Account* having served its first purpose, he began to recast his translated narratives for the quarto *Historical Collection.* The *Account* he eventually released in 1769 after Bougainville's return in March.[64]

The question arises as to whether the *Account* as privately issued in 1767 differed in any respect from that formally published in 1769. Though all known copies appear to date from 1769, there are reasons for suggesting that the two issues differed in the form of the preface. Pages i to xii describe Dalrymple hopeful of employment in the expedition; from page xii to page xv the tone is of disappointed hopes. Pages xii to xv do not apply to Dalrymple's 1767 situation, and the *Account* cannot have circulated in 1767 in this form.[65] No copy has been identified as dating from 1767, although the separated 'Chart of the South Pacifick Ocean' in Joseph Banks' map collection is from a preliminary state of the plate without engraved title, and bears marks of having been folded into an octavo volume.[66] It may come from an early issue of the *Account,* though there was no copy of the *Account* inventoried when Banks' library was delivered to the British Museum in 1827.[67] No other copy of the chart is known to have survived from this preliminary state, either loose or bound into a copy of the *Account.*

Dalrymple noted that Banks 'carried with him [on *Endeavour*] the 8° *"Account of the Discoveries made in the So. Pacific Ocean,"* with the *Chart,* which I had printed several months before':[68] this suggests a copy of the 1767 issue. Banks' journal twice notes a page reference and a description of a plate in the *Account,* suggesting that the main text was unchanged between the 1767 and 1769 issues.[69] The *Account* is one of few books mentioned by Banks or Cook as a source used on *Endeavour.*

Dalrymple's 'Chart of the South Pacifick Ocean', present in the *Account* on *Endeavour,* provided the historical background, rather than navigational information, for Cook's decision to seek and pass through Torres Strait. Cook used de Brosses' *Histoire des navigations* as his chief source at this point,[70] though the text gave no authority for the depiction of a strait on Robert de Vaugondy's maps. The maps themselves showed no expedition tracks, and only conjectured the separate coastlines east of the Dutch discoveries in the Gulf of Carpentaria. Dalrymple had entered on his chart the tracks of all the voyages he discussed, continuing Torres' track south of New Guinea, even though the text of the *Account* stopped short of the New Hebrides. Though he cited Arias' memorial as a source for Quiros' and Torres' voyage generally, it was outside the terms of reference of the *Account* (p. xix) to describe Torres' coasting of southern New Guinea. But he gave Banks information from Arias' memorial relating to Torres' track and was assured that this had governed the decision.

> Torres' track, which I had laid down in my Chart from Arias's memorial, determined the Endeavour to pass between New Holland and New Guinea; there were great differences of opinion on the subject; Captain Cook insisted, on the authority of Pingré, that Torres had passed to the Northward of New Guinea, Mr. Banks maintained that he had kept it on his right hand; the Track in my chart

decided the point; and, Mr. Banks, the very first time I saw him after his return to England, quoted the words of Arias's memorial, which he could have got only from me.[71]

In consequence the *Account* was prominent in the pamphlet skirmish which erupted briefly in 1773 over the imaginative rendering of Cook's and Banks' journals in Hawkesworth's *Voyages,*[72] in which Dalrymple found himself accused by Hawkesworth of misrepresenting the Spanish and Dutch Pacific voyages in support of his own theories. In *A Letter from Mr. Dalrymple to Dr. Hawkesworth,* he published long extracts from the *Account* in rebuttal, and promised to print Arias' memorial in Spanish as evidence.[73] Never one to tread lightly on the sensibilities of others, Dalrymple criticised Hawkesworth further for producing a literary work rather than a scientific account. Hawkesworth rushed out a 'Preface to the Second Edition', and only his untimely death terminated the quarrel.[74]

Dalrymple's dispute was with Hawkesworth the editor, not with Cook. On hearing news of Cook's discovery of New Zealand, he had conceived, with Benjamin Franklin, a speculative scheme for a settlement there.[75] He offered to assist Hawkesworth in preparing the views and log-book extracts of Cook's voyage for publication, an offer as genuine as it was misunderstood.[76] Much later, in 1784, Dalrymple was one of the collaborators (though not without incident) in the publication of Cook's journal of his third voyage.[77] His interest in the new discoveries transcended any passing disappointment of 1768.

The *Account* and the *Historical Collection*

Though Dalrymple cited the *Account* against Hawkesworth in 1773, he had by then superseded the edition (though not the arguments) with the *Historical Collection*. In 1769, as well as publishing the *Account,* Dalrymple had also reused its elements in the quarto *Historical Collection,* which had as its basis the translated narratives of the Spanish and Dutch voyages. He published the Spanish voyages with introductory memoirs (including 'Data on which the Chart of the South-Sea was formed') as the first volume in 1769, perhaps as early as September, but quickly reissued it with a changed title-page and dedication early in 1770.[78] The second volume, for the Dutch voyages, he published in two fascicles in 1771, with the second and third sections of the *Account,* 'Conduct of the Discoverers' and 'Investigation of what may be farther expected', and 'A Chronological Table of Discoveries', reprinted without significant change as supplementary articles. The main 'Geographical Description' he withdrew, to await revision with the publication of the voyages of Byron, Carteret, Wallis, Bougainville and Cook.

The demise of the *Account* was unspectacular. In an advertisement which appeared with the temporary title-page of the first fascicle of the second volume of *Historical Collection,* Dalrymple announced: 'The Purchasers of *An Account of the Discoveries in the South Pacifick Ocean, previous to 1764,* 8vo. on returning that Tract before the Conclusion of the second Volume [of the *Historical Collection*] may have their Money allowed in the Price of these Volumes.' Many purchasers apparently did so, though the *Account* was not formally withdrawn from sale. Dalrymple's London agent John Nourse held the remaining stock of 106 copies in 1775, for sale at 1s.6d. each, and he and his successor Francis Wingrave disposed of five further copies before returning the remainder of 101 copies to Dalrymple in 1794.[79] A recent worldwide survey of public, academic and private collections has recorded only twenty-two surviving copies, four of which are in Australia.

The *Account of the Discoveries* marks a watershed in the history of the exploration of the southern hemisphere. Dalrymple searched out and analysed the knowledge gained in exploration over 200 years, putting forward the argument for a 'great southern continent' with such vigour that the settling of the questions he raised was made the second prime purpose of the expedition he had hoped to lead. It was the theory pressed by Dalrymple which caused the Admiralty to give Cook instructions to sail south from Tahiti to 40° South, and west to locate the east coast of New Zealand, before coming home. But it was Cook's idea to cross Tasman's track and to run northwards along the east coast of Australia to try to verify the existence of Torres Strait. The voyage of *Endeavour* changed the concept of exploration from historical analysis to scientific investigation. Dalrymple, having disqualified himself from the expedition, was to pursue the analytical line, as hydrographer for the East India Company and the Admiralty, for more than forty years more. He was elected to the Royal Society in 1771 as 'a Gentleman well versed in Mathematical & Geographical knowledge, & translator of Voyages to the South Seas & other places, from Spanish'.[80]

But for a short time at the end of the 1760s he spanned the divide, and set the exploration agenda which sent Cook to the South Pacific and Australia three times in nine years on voyages of discovery.

N O T E S

[1] Biographical information is from Andrew S. Cook, 'An Author Voluminous and Vast': Alexander Dalrymple (1737-1808), Hydrographer to the East India Company and to the Admiralty, as Publisher: A Catalogue of Books and Charts, Ph.D. thesis, St Andrews, 1992.

[2] 'Memoirs of Alexander Dalrymple, Esq.', The *European Magazine and London Review* 42, 1802, pp. 323-328, *321-*327, and 421-424.

[3] For Dalrymple's Borneo, Philippines, Celebes and South China Sea voyages, see Howard T. Fry, *Alexander Dalrymple (1737-1808) and the Expansion of British Trade,* London, 1970; Nicholas Tarling, *Sulu and Sabah: A Study of British Policy towards the Philippines and North Borneo,* Kuala Lumpur, 1978, ch. 1; Vincent T. Harlow, *The Founding of the Second British Empire 1763-1793,* vol. I, London, 1952, pp. 70-83.

[4] Dalrymple received from his brother David on 7 October 1765 money due from their father's estate (National Library of Scotland, Edinburgh, MS. 25283, ff. 84-85 [Newhailes Papers]).

[5] 'Memoirs of Alexander Dalrymple', p. 327.

[6] For the development of European knowledge of the Pacific Ocean, see Lawrence C. Wroth, 'The Early Cartography of the Pacific', *Papers of the Bibliographical Society of America* 38, 1944, pp. 87-268 (reprinted New York, 1963). For the Australian coast, see Glyndwr Williams and Alan Frost, *Terra Australis to Australia,* Melbourne, 1988, chs 3 and 4.

[7] Andrew Sharp, *The Discovery of the Pacific Islands,* Oxford, 1960.

[8] Lord Amherst of Hackney and Basil Thomson, *The Discovery of the Solomon Islands by Alvaro de Mendaña in 1568,* 2 vols, Hakluyt Society, 1901.

[9] Markham, *The Voyages of Pedro Fernandez de Quiros, 1595-1606,* 2 vols, Hakluyt Society, 1904. A report from Quiros was copied by de Morga: J. S. Cummins, *Sucesos de las Islas Filipinas by Antonio de Morga,* Hakluyt Society, 1971, pp. 97-105.

[10] Markham, *The Voyages of Pedro Fernandez de Quiros;* Celsus Kelly, *La Austrialia del Espiritu Santo: The Journal of Fray Martin de Munilla O.F.M. and other documents relating to the Voyage of Pedro Fernandez de Quiros to the South Sea (1605-1606) ...,* 2 vols, Hakluyt Society, 1966. For the Spanish voyages, particularly analysis of Quiros' reports, see also Colin Jack-Hinton, *The Search for the Islands of Solomon 1567-1838,*

Oxford, 1969; Celsus Kelly, *Calendar of Documents: Spanish Voyages in the South Pacific from Alvaro de Mendaña to Alejandro Malaspina 1567-1794* ..., Madrid, 1965.

[11] Andrew Sharp, *The Discovery of Australia,* Oxford, 1963, particularly pp. 23-30; Henry N. Stevens, *New Light on the Discovery of Australia,* Hakluyt Society, 1930.

[12] W. A. Engelbrecht and P. J. van Herwerden, *De Ontdekkingsreis van Jacob Le Maire en Willem Cornelisz. Schouten in de Jaren 1615-1617,* The Hague, 1945.

[13] Andrew Sharp, *The Voyages of Abel Janszoon Tasman,* Oxford, 1968.

[14] Andrew Sharp, *The Journal of Jacob Roggeveen,* Oxford, 1970.

[15] Colin Jack-Hinton, 'Alexander Dalrymple and the Rediscovery of the Islands of Solomon', *The Mariner's Mirror* 50, 1964, pp. 93-114; Jack-Hinton, *The Search for the Islands of Solomon;* and Kelly, *Calendar of Documents.*

[16] Antonio de Herrera y Tordesillas, *Descripcion de las Indias Ocidentales,* Madrid, 1601, appended to his *Historia General de los Hechos de los Castellanos en las Islas i Tierre Firme del Mar Oceano,* 4 vols, Madrid, 1601-1616. Dalrymple used the 1728 folio edition.

[17] Antonio de Morga, *Sucesos de las Islas Filipinas,* Mexico, 1609, ff. 33v-39v; Melchisedec Thevenot, *Relations des divers voyages curieux,* Paris, 1696, vol. ii, appendix. Dalrymple acquired a copy of Christoval Suarez de Figueroa, *Hechos de Don García Hurtado de Mendoza cuarto Marqués de Cañete,* Madrid, 1613, only in 1769 (see note 29).

[18] J. de Torquemada, *Monarchia Indiana con el Origen y Guerras de las Indias Occidentales,* 3 vols, Madrid, 1723. Quiros' memorials to King Philip III of Spain were the 'Eighth Memorial' and the January 1609 memorial, both in English translation in Samuel Purchas, *Hakluytus Posthumus or Purchas His Pilgrimes* ..., 5 vols, London, 1624-1626, vol. iv, pp. 1422-1432. For the 'Eighth Memorial' Dalrymple knew also a Spanish manuscript which he collated with the 1613 Amsterdam Latin edition (Kelly, *Calendar of Documents,* pp. 243 and 248).

[19] *Journal ofte Beschryvinghe van de Wonderlicke Reyse, ghedaen door Willem Cornelisz. Schouten van Hoorn,* Amsterdam, 1618; *Spieghel der Australische Navigatie door den Wijt vermaerden ende cloeckmoedighen Zee-Heldt, Iacob Le Maire* ..., Amsterdam, 1622. Jack-Hinton, *The Search for the Islands of Solomon,* pp. 190-191, deals with the complex bibliography of this voyage.

[20]François Valentijn, *Oud en Nieuw Oost-Indiën,* 5 vols, Dordrecht, 1724-1726, vol. iii, part ii, pp. 47-58.

[21]*Tweejarige Reyse rondom de Wereld,* Dordrecht, 1728; C. F. Behrens, *Histoire de l'expedition de trois vaisseaux ... aux terres australes en MDCCXXI,* 2 vols, The Hague, 1739. Dalrymple was unaware that both embroidered considerably the basic *Kort en Nauwkeurig Verhaal van de Reize der Drie Schepen in 't Jaar 1721 ...,* Amsterdam, 1727.

[22]Charles de Brosses, *Histoire des navigations aux terres australes,* 2 vols, Paris, 1756. For Dalrymple's correspondence with de Brosses, see Alan Carey Taylor, *Le Président de Brosses et l'Australie,* Paris, 1937, pp. 157-159. A free English translation of the *Histoire* (with copies of two of Robert de Vaugondy's maps, but without the chronological table) was published in 3 volumes by John Callander as *Terra Australis Cognita,* Edinburgh, 1766.

[23]Alexander Dalrymple, *Catalogue of Authors who have written on Rio de la Plata,* London, 1807, p. 16: 'Above 40 years ago I purchased from Mr. Thomas Davies, Russel Street, Covent Garden, 2 Volumes of Spanish printed Memorials and MSS, which had belonged to the celebrated M. Colbert, the French Minister.'

[24]R. H. Major, *Early Voyages to Terra Australis,* Hakluyt Society, 1859, pp. 1-30; Markham, *The Voyages of Pedro Fernandez de Quiros,* vol. ii, pp. 517-536. See also Kelly, *Calendar of Documents,* pp. 329-31; Howard T. Fry, 'Alexander Dalrymple and New Guinea', *Journal of Pacific History* 4, 1969, pp. 83-104, particularly pp. 85-86.

[25]The *Relacion* of 12 July 1607 sent by Torres from Manila to King Philip III is described by Kelly, *Calendar of Documents,* pp. 213-214. The text was copied for Dalrymple by Juan Bautista Munoz in the Spanish archives at Simancas in October 1782, and Dalrymple's translation published by James Burney, *A Chronological History of the Discoveries in the South Sea or Pacific Ocean,* 5 vols, London, 1803-1817, vol. ii, pp. 272 and 467-478. See also note 27 below.

[26]Tasman had expected, in 1643, to find a passage from the north coast of New Guinea to the Arafura Sea and, for his 1644 voyage, he was instructed to search again by approaching eastward along the south coast of New Guinea (Sharp, *The Voyages of Abel Janszoon Tasman,* pp. 219-223 and 313-314).

[27]Alexander Dalrymple, *Considerations on M. Buache's Memoir concerning New Britain and the North Coast of New Guinea,* London, 1790, p. ii: 'Early in Life I saw, at Madrass a Spanish MS of these parts;

which, to the best of my recollection, contained the Discoveries of Torres in 1606 on the South of New-Guinea, It was amongst the Papers of Mr. William Roberts, who had been a Supra Cargo to Manila, and who lost his life in the siege of Madrass, but on my return there in 1762, after my first Voyage to Sooloo, I in vain endeavoured to trace it: I am assured that the Original letter of Torres, dated at Manila 12th July 1607, is still existing in Spain.' Dalrymple normally used 'MS' or 'manuscript' to denote a manuscript *map* or *chart;* text documents he usually categorised as 'letter', 'account', 'relation', 'memorial', etc. One should not infer that he had known of a *text* account of Torres' voyage at Madras in 1759. (In replying to criticism by the French geographer J. P. Buache de la Neuville of his 1760s deductions about the islands north-east of New Guinea, he was being 'economical with the truth' over his knowledge of the Torres letter.)

28Dalrymple taught himself both French and Spanish while at Madras ('Memoirs of Alexander Dalrymple', pp. 325-327).

29For each voyage Dalrymple introduced substantial translated extracts relevant to his argument, but the translated texts of the two Quiros memorials he gave in full as separate sections (Alexander Dalrymple, *An Historical Collection of the Several Voyages and Discoveries in the South Pacific Ocean,* 2 vols, London, 1769/70-71, vol. 1, pp. 145-174). He included extracts from his newly acquired Figueroa (see note 17 above) as a postscript dated September 1769 (pp. 175-204).

30Dalrymple, *Historical Collection,* vol. i, pp. xiv-xvi.

31By 'Papua' Dalrymple meant New Guinea. He also omitted from the *Account* the islands immediately east of New Guinea (p. xix), though he was to deal with them in *Historical Collection* in 1769 (vol. i, pp. 16-21: 'Of the Salomon Islands').

32Didier Robert de Vaugondy, Carte générale qui réprésente les Mers des Indes, Pacifique, et Atlantique, et principalement le Monde Austral ..., Paris, 1756.

33Guillaume Delisle, Hemisphere Meridionale pour voir plus distinctement les Terres Australes, Paris, 1714; J. N. Bellin, Carte reduite des mers comprises entre l'Asie et l'Amerique ..., Paris, 1742, and 'Observations sur la construction de la carte des mers comprises entre l'Asie et l'Amerique', *Mémoires pour l'histoire des sciences & de beaux arts,* Paris, 1742, pp. 866-894 and 942-971. Some of Bellin's improvements were incorporated in John Green [Bradock Mead], A Chart of North America and South America, including the Atlantic and Pacific Oceans ..., London, 1753, and discussed by him in *Remarks, in support of the New*

Chart of North and South America, London, 1753, pp. 43-44. Robert
de Vaugondy appears to have used Green as one of his sources.

[34] Dalrymple, *Historical Collection,* vol. i, pp. 1-15. The chart appears both
in the *Account* and in the *Historical Collection,* and the explanation in
'Data' also serves here.

[35] Adam Smith to Earl of Shelburne, 12 February 1767, National Library of
Scotland, Edinburgh, Acc. 11142; published in E. C. Mossner and I. S.
Ross, *The Correspondence of Adam Smith,* Oxford, 1977, pp. 122-124,
no. 101; formerly in the Marquis of Lansdowne's archive at Bowood
House, Wiltshire, and sold at Christie's, London, 12 October 1994, lot 76.
Dalrymple had already written to de Brosses, who replied on 18 February
1767: 'Je suis charmé d'apprendre que vous travaillez a rassembler tous ce
que nous avons de connoissances geographiques, historiques, et naturelles
sur le mer du sud et la partie du globe que dans mon ouvrage j'ai appellé
Polynesie; j'ai beaucoup d'empressement de voir votre ouvrage aussi-tot
que vous le ferez paroitre.' (Dalrymple, *Historical Collection,* vol. i,
p. xxxii).

[36] Dalrymple to Earl of Chatham, 24 November 1766, Public Record
Office, London, PRO.30/8/31, f. 11 [Chatham Papers].

[37] 'Memoirs of Alexander Dalrymple', pp. *324-*325.

[38] Helen Wallis, *Carteret's Voyage round the World,* 2 vols, Hakluyt
Society, 1965. For Wallis' voyage, see Hugh Carrington, *The Discovery of
Tahiti,* Hakluyt Society, 1948.

[39] Wallis, *Carteret's Voyage,* vol. ii, pp. 302-306, no. 34.

[40] Resolution of 5 June 1766 (Royal Society, London, Council Minute
Book V, 1763-1768, pp. 155-156).

[41] Harry Woolf, *The Transits of Venus: A Study of Eighteenth-Century
Science,* Princeton, 1959, particularly pp. 16-19.

[42] E. Halley, 'A particular method by which the parallax of the Sun, or its
distance from the Earth, may be ascertained by the assistance of the
Transit of Venus over the Sun', *Philosophical Transactions of the Royal
Society* 29, 1716, pp. 454-464.

[43] Derek Howse, *Nevil Maskelyne: The Seaman's Astronomer,* Cambridge,
1989, pp. 18-40.

[44] Thomas Hornsby, 'On the Transit of Venus in 1769', *Philosophical
Transactions of the Royal Society* 55, 1765, pp. 326-344. Hornsby's paper
was read on 13 February 1766.

[45]See page 24 and note 33 for discussions of Delisle's map.

[46]Royal Society: Journal Books, 1766-1767; Letters & Papers L&P.IV.405. Dalrymple published his paper in 1769 in *Historical Collection,* vol. i, pp. 22-24, as 'An Enquiry into the Formation of Islands'.

[47]Royal Society, Council Minute Book V, p. 184. A copy was later made of minutes concerning the Transit of Venus expedition (Royal Society, Manuscripts MS.647).

[48]Royal Society, Council Minute Book V, pp. 193-207. Short typified the general uncertainty by advising the ships to 'endeavour to find some Land, or Islands in the said [South] Seas', and recommended: 'This search should begin about 50° degrees of Longitude to the West of the Western Coast of South America, and may be continued for 70° degrees further to the West, and should be between the Equator and 25° of South Latitude. In this space a great Number of Islands are set down in the Maps, and any of them will do very well for this purpose.'

[49]Royal Society, Council Minute Book V, pp. 187-189.

[50]Royal Society, Council Minute Book V, pp. 207-209. The other candidates were Dunn, Dymond, Green and Wales, of whom Dymond and Green were former assistant observers at Greenwich. Maskelyne reported, at the time of the council resolution, that Dalrymple, Dunn and Wales had already expressed willingness to be candidates.

[51]Royal Society, Miscellaneous Manuscripts MM.3.14.

[52]Dalrymple, *Historical Collection,* vol. i, pp. vii-viii.

[53]The 'publication' date of October 1767 on the chart provides the earliest date for issue of the *Account.*

[54]Alexander Dalrymple, *A Letter from Mr. Dalrymple to Dr. Hawkesworth* ..., London, 1773, pp. 28-29.

[55]See notes 35, 36 and 51. To Chatham in November 1766 he wrote: 'I am not insensible, notwithstanding the instances of Dampier, Halley, &ca. how foreign to rules of Office it is, to form the most distant expectation, that a person may be employ'd in the publick service by sea, who has no rank in the Navy.' To Morton at the Royal Society he wrote on 7 December 1767: 'I have no Thoughts of undertaking the Voyage, as a Passenger going out to make the Observations, or on any other footing, than that of having the management of the Ship intended for the Service.'

[56]Royal Society, Council Minute Book V, pp. 38-39. The Earl of Morton

reported, at the 3 April meeting, that he had recommended Dalrymple 'according to his letter [of 7 December]'.

[57]'Memoirs of Alexander Dalrymple', p. *325. Harold B. Carter, 'The Royal Society and the Voyage of HMS *Endeavour* 1768-71', *Notes and Records of the Royal Society of London* 49, 1995, pp. 245-260, particularly pp. 251-254. The Navy Board order for the survey of the vessels was issued on 23 March (Fry, *Alexander Dalrymple,* p. 119).

[58]Royal Society, Council Minute Book V, pp. 38-39. Dalrymple recorded that 'offers were made to [him] that the instructions for the voyage would be entrusted to him, and the Officer commanding the vessel be positively ordered to follow his opinion' ('Memoirs of Alexander Dalrymple', p. *325).

[59]Royal Society, Manuscripts MS.633 (Council rough minute book).

[60]28 April, 14 July and 4 August 1768 (Royal Society, Royal Society Club Dinner Book 5). Dalrymple had dined on 10 March as the guest of the President.

[61]Draft letter from Morton to Philip Stephens, Admiralty (Royal Society, Council Minute Book V, pp. 335-337). In case Tahiti was not found, Maskelyne provided a reserve 'Table of the limits of Latitude and Longitude, within which it is proper to observe the next transit of Venus', which was incorporated in the expedition instructions.

[62]*A Letter from Mr. Dalrymple,* p. 2. Banks went on board the *Endeavour* on 25 August (Harold B. Carter, *Sir Joseph Banks 1743-1820,* London, 1988, pp. 67 and 73).

[63]The copy in the Royal Library, Windsor Castle, in a contemporary full leather binding, but without marks of provenance.

[64]Dalrymple, *Historical Collection,* vol. i, p. vii; *A Letter from Mr. Dalrymple,* p. 2.

[65]The printer's signatures for the preliminary pages of the 1769 issue give the collation formula π^2 A^{8}a^8 before B-G^8 H^4 for the main text. This is unusual, and suggests a preface modified and extended from 16 pages (A^8) to 32 pages (A^{8}a^8) after the original issue. Dalrymple reworked the material again in 1769 for the preface of *Historical Collection,* vol. i.

[66]British Library: Maps 181.m.1. America, no. 50.

[67]British Library: 460.g.1.

[68]*A Letter from Mr. Dalrymple,* p. 2.

[69]J. C. Beaglehole, *The Endeavour Journal of Joseph Banks 1768-1771,*

2 vols, Sydney, 1962, vol. i, p. 400 ('as represented in Mr Dalrymple's book p. 63'), and vol. ii, p. 16 ('as is represented in Mr Dalrymple's account of Tasmans Voyage, in a plat which I beleive is copied from Valentynes history'). Dalrymple had 6 plates re-engraved from Valentijn, *Oud en Nieuw Oost-Indiën,* intending them to be bound at various points between pages 62 and 68 to illustrate his summary of Tasman's voyage. Banks was describing features of the plate of 'Murderers Bay', bound facing page 63 in his copy. An alternative binding order, followed in the copy reprinted here, places all 6 illustrations at the end of the text. In two further places in his journal (vol. i, pp. 209 and 240) Banks writes from a direct examination of the chart in the *Account.*

[70] J. C. Beaglehole, *The Journals of Captain James Cook,* 3 vols, Hakluyt Society, 1955-1974, vol. i, p. 410 (and see also pp. cliv-clxiv).

[71] *A Letter from Mr. Dalrymple,* p. 29.

[72] John Hawkesworth, *An Account of the Voyages ... for making Discoveries in the Southern Hemisphere,* 3 vols, London, 1773.

[73] The untitled text, beginning 'SEÑOR. El Doctor Iuan Luis Arias, dize: Que por conuenir ...' and occupying 28 quarto pages, was printed in 1773 in Edinburgh by Murray and Cochrane.

[74] Dalrymple prepared two versions of *Mr. Dalrymple's Observations on Dr. Hawkesworth's Preface to the Second Edition* in September 1773, but the issue was stopped when Hawkesworth died in November (Sir Maurice Holmes, *Captain James Cook: A Bibliographical Excursion,* London, 1952, pp. 22-25; John Lawrence Abbott, *John Hawkesworth: Eighteenth-Century Man of Letters,* Madison, 1982, ch 7).

[75] [Alexander Dalrymple,] 'The Country called, in the Maps, New Zealand ...', London, 1771.

[76] *A Letter from Mr. Dalrymple,* p. 33.

[77] Helen Wallis, 'Publication of Cook's Journals: Some New Sources and Assessments', *Pacific Studies* 1, 1978, pp. 163-194.

[78] An intermediate issue retains the 1769 dedication, but cancels the 1769 half-title and title-page alone with a specially set half-sheet dated 1770. The three issues differ only in the preliminary pages: from page ix to the end of the volume all issues are from the same sheet stock.

[79] Royal Astronomical Society, London, Add. MS. 5.13-15 (Miscellaneous papers of John Nourse).

[80] Royal Society, Certificates 1767-1778 III, 14 February 1771.

A N
A C C O U N T

OF THE

D I S C O V E R I E S

MADE IN THE

South Pacifick Ocean,

Previous to 1764.

AN

ACCOUNT

OF THE

DISCOVERIES

MADE IN THE

SOUTH PACIFICK OCEAN,

Previous to 1764.

PART I.

CONTAINING,

I. A Geographical Defcription of Places.

II. An Examination of the Conduct of the Difcoverers in the Tracks they purfued.

III. Inveftigations of what may be further expected.

Tierra que fica onde
Com fuas frias Afas o Auftro a efconde.
CAMOEN's LUSIADA, Canto 10. S. 11.

LONDON:
Printed in the Year 1767.

THE

PREFACE.

THAT Genoese who, in the service of Spain, attempted, and that Portuguese who, in the same service, effected the circumnavigation of the globe, have precluded all competition in the honour of *sublime* discovery. Much, however, is still within the power of men who may be rather emulous of the glorious spirit of that age, than devoted to the mercenary or indolent disposition of the present. However, even in that age of enterprize their proffers were undervalued at home: and altho' they were heard with more atten-

A   tion

tion abroad, perhaps, America would have remained ſtill undiſcovered, had not Queen Iſabella, with unequal'd publick virtue, pledged her own jewels to equip Columbus.

The ſame motive which carried Columbus and Magellan into foreign countries, in ſome meaſure, induces the Author of the following ſheets to publiſh them to the world.

General geography and diſcoveries have almoſt from infancy been the fond object of his attention. And altho' he went to the Eaſt-Indies, in the ſervice of the Company, at an early age, neither the circum-

circumftances of life in which he was placed, the difpofition of his companions, nor the want of books, could over-rule the natural propenfity of his mind.

Every young man enters life with a paffion to emulate thofe characters which have gained his admiration. In moft men the rubs of life foon blunt this paffion; in fome it prevails over all difficulties.

The Author looking up to Columbus, to Magellan, and to thofe immortal heroes who have difplay'd new worlds to our view, and extended the European name and influence amongft diftant nations, was inflamed with the ambition to do *fomething* to promote the general benefit of mankind, at the fame time that it fhould add to the glory and intereft of his country.

The firft and moft ftriking object of refearch was, The difcovery of a Southern Continent. But from want of lights to follow, tho' the defire was early fixed in his breaft, other objects intervened, and many years paffed without any determined purfuit towards that quarter.

The defire of information having led him to examine the old records at Madrafs. He foon found from them, that the Company, in antient times, placed a great value on the

com-

commerce to the Eastern Islands, and were very solicitous to regain a portion of it after they were deprived thereof by the intrigues of the Dutch, and the pusilanimity of our own court. From an examination of the Company's records, and from the printed accounts of our early voyages, he was led to the persuasion, that this valuable branch of commerce might not only be regained but extended much beyond what it ever was. Fully convinced of the great importance of this object, the Author, in the beginning of 1759, declined a distinguished employment at Fort St. George (that of Secretary), and had the direction of a small vessel of the Company's intended for the

A 3   service

service he had proposed. From
that time, till the end of 1764,
he made several voyages in different
vessels to the Eastern parts, thro'
seas unknown, and amongst people
with whom we had before no in-
tercourse. Altho', from the very
involved situation of the Company's affairs, and from the dif-
sentions at home, the great national
advantages, which these voyages
pointed out, have not hitherto been
vigorously pursued: yet the Company in several letters to India, expressed their approbation of his
conduct.

However warmly this object may
have been pursued, the Author
never lost sight of the great Paf-
sion

sion of his life. Above eight years ago he made a collection of the voyages into the South Sea, of which he could find any intimation in the English books to be met with in India. This collection was indeed imperfect; but an active mind, long employed on any subject, will acquire ideas from very faint lines. His peregrinations were of use to him even in this pursuit; for his attention being awake, in the research so natural to that curiosity, he acquired, amongst the Spaniards, some very valuable papers, and intimations from Spanish writers, many of whose works he also procured.

A 4 On

On the Author's return to Europe, he was induced to forego every wish towards objects perhaps more lucrative, tho' less magnanimous, and was solicitous to be engaged on discovery in the South-Sea. For which kind of undertaking he presumed to think himself, in some measure, qualified from five years experience in such like voyages, and from long attention to the subject.

However, to recommend himself to this employment, so much wished for, and conscious, *previous to any new undertaking*, how necessary it was to know what had been done in former times, lest on the return from a tedious and expensive voyage, he should betray his own ignorance,

PREFACE.

rance, by having *only* trodden in
the fteps of fome *difcoverer*; he
determined to make an hiftorical
collection of all the difcoveries in
the South-Sea; as well from the circumftances he could find in old
printed books, as from thofe to be
met with only in the Spanifh papers he had acquired. Very fortunately, after his return to England,
he obtained a curious collection of
Spanifh memorials: thefe greatly
elucidate the printed relations,
which, without this affiftance, muft
have remained unintelligible. Having tranflated the feveral relations
he could procure, and reduced
them to a chronological order, the
Author, from thefe materials, drew
up a fummary defcription of the
places

places hitherto difcovered in the South-Sea.

The *Southern Continent* having been feen on the Weft-fide, by Taf-man, in 1642, and on the Eaft by Juan Fernandes above half a century before, and by others after him, in different latitudes, from 64° to 40° S. It is impoffible for any one at this time to *difcover* it. But the extenfive countries intermediate, equal in extent to all the civilifed part of Afia, from Turkey to China inclufive, ftill remain unexplored. And altho' the land has been feen, and once vifited, yet to open an intercourfe with its inhabitants, is a tafk ftill to be performed.

In-

Intrepidity, joined to every naval accomplifhment, is not adequate to this tafk. To execute it effectually, not only a knowledge of what has been done, and a retrofpect to whatever is worthy imitation, or blameable in paft difcoverers, are requifite; but alfo a philofophick idea of winds and feafons; a freedom from prejudice; attention to the temper and difpofition of men in their uncultivated ftate; and, perhaps, not lefs than all, a confideration of the rights and value of man's life, to fecure a patient abftinence from the ufe of fire-arms againft the native Indians, who muft be ignorant of the intentions and language of the difcoverer.

Where

Where fo much is required, it may, perhaps, be impoſſible to find the fit leader; but in ſuch circumſtances, the idea of *fitneſs* ariſes from compariſon.

The Author having been difappointed in his hopes, is under the neceſſity to forego all thoughts of being employed in the manner he wiſhed, either immediately in the ſervice of the government, or in that of the Eaſt-India company: but, at the ſame time, the leaſt he could do, in juſtice to the public and to himſelf, was to communicate to the world what lights he had acquired, and what deductions he had formed, on a ſubject ſo important; and he ſhall be happy if

his

his labours may hereafter conduce, in the fmalleft degree, to the general advantage of mankind, and to his country in particular : Indeed, he fhall think his pains amply rewarded, if thefe fheets are inftrumental in faving the life of *one* Indian from the deftruction occafioned by impatience.

It appears from the following fheets, that not only many large Iflands, and fmall ones without number, fwarming with people, are fcattered over the South Pacifick Ocean, but that it is more than probable another Continent will be there found extending from about 30° S. towards the Pole.

There

There can be no doubt that countries so well situated, so extensive, and so full of civilized inhabitants, must afford a very beneficial commerce: so that considered, either from the advantages immediately to be derived from thence, or as a barrier to secure the trade of the East-Indies, the examination of the countries situated in the South Pacifick Ocean, seemed to be an object of great consequence to the Company.

Having mentioned a few words of the motives which led the Author to this Study, and how solicitous he was to be employed in carrying his ideas into execution, it remains to explain the nature of

the work here offered to the attention of the publick, and the materials from which it is compofed.

The objeƈt of the prefent difquifition being confined to the Ocean,
comprehended between South America and Papua, nothing beyond
thefe limits, or to the North of
the Equator, will be inferted, un-
lefs where it is requifite thereby to
to regulate a fituation.

This work contains two parts.

The firft (now publifhed) com-
prehends as full and diftinƈt an account of the lands in the South-Seas
as the circumftances mentioned in

the

the original relations will, from an
attentive confideration, admit.

The fecond is an hiftorical collection of the feveral voyages acrofs
the South Pacifick Ocean in a chronological feries.

In the firft part the plan laid
down is to give,

1. A Geographical Defcription
of the places hitherto difcovered
between America and Papua on
the South of the Equator.

2. It is propofed to examine
into the Conduct of the Difcoverers
in the Tracks they made choice
of. And having thus recapitulated
every

PREFACE. xvii

every thing that has been difcovered,

3. It is in view to inveftigate
what may be farther expected, in
this quarter, from the analogy of
nature, as well as from the deduction of paft difcoveries.

The fituations in this geographical defcription are fuch as, from a
full difcuffion of all circumftances
mentioned in the original authors,
appear to be the moft probable :
but no aftronomical obfervations of
longitude having hitherto been
made, to determine the fituation of
any of thefe places, or even to regulate the weftern limit; it is far

a from

from being imagined their fituations attain a minute precifion.

It was thought proper that the reafons for the determination of fituations fhould be given apart: this is done in the fection entitled, " Data, on which the chart of the " South-Sea was formed ;" to this fection they muſt recur who are folicitous to enter into a critical examination of the map.

It is meant that the geographical defcription fhall comprehend as full an account of the inhabitants and productions of the places it mentions, as the intimations we have will admit : and for this pur-pofe the words of the original are

com-

commonly preferved. But as the places difcovered between America and Papua do not all lead to the great object of this difquifition,

A SOUTHERN CONTINENT,

it is meant to poftpone the defcription of the Iflands and Countries towards Papua, and only to give an account of all thofe which lie between America and the interfection of Schouten's track by Tafman's.

In the fecond part, which contains the hiftorical collection of the feveral voyages acrofs the South Pacifick Ocean, in a chronological feries, the tranflations are almoft literal, which was preferred to a more polifhed ftile, left any devi-

ation

ation from the expreffion of the original fhould introduce ambiguity, or render the authenticity fufpected. Where the meaning appeared doubtful, an afterifk is placed in the margin, and the original paffage commonly inferted at the bottom of the page.

Perhaps, hereafter, this collection may be extended to the feveral intimations we have of New-Britain, formerly called the Salomon Iflands, New-Guinea, and the other parts of Papua; and even to comprehend the Iflands from thence to the Ladrones or Marianes.

It may be ufeful, at leaft it will be fatisfactory, to give a brief recital of the voyages and the authorities from whence they are taken.

1520.

	Herrera,	Ramufio,	Baros,
1520. Hernando Magellanes,	D. 2. L. 9. ch. 15.	Vol. I. p. 355. Edit. 1563. D. 3. L. 5, ch. 10. Edit. 1628.	
1537. Ferdinand Grijalva, and Alvarado,	Ditto, D. 7. L. 5. ch. 9.	Ditto, D. 5. L. 6. ch. 5.	De Couto, D. 5. L. 6. ch. 5.
1567. Alvaro de Mendoça,	Ditto,	Galvano,	Argensola, L. 2. p. 64.
Alvaro Mendana de Neyra,	Juan Louis Arias's Memorial.	Descripcion de las Indias, p. 56.	
15 Ditto,	Ditto.		
1575. Ditto,	Ditto,	Ovalle, p. 65.	
Circiter 1576. Juan Fernandes,	Ditto.		
1595. Alvaro Mendana de Neyra,	Quiros's Letter to Morga,	Churchill's Collect. V. 5. p. 695.	
1599. Theodore Gerrards,	Purchas, Vol. IV. p. 1391. note.	Barleus's Collect. p. 193.	
1606. Pedro Fernandes de Quiros, and Louis Vaez de Torres,	Torquemada, V. I. L. 5. ch. 64.	Arias, Quiros's Memorials. Arias.	
1616. James Le Maire and W. Schouten,	Janson, 4to. 1618.	Barleus, fol. 1622.	
1624. Orange, one of the Naffau fleet.			
1642. Abel Janfan Tafman,	Valentyn, Vol. III.	De Hondt, Thevenot, Campbell's Collect. Hooke's Phil. Collect.	
1687. John Davis,	Wafer,	Dampier.	
1722. Jacob Roggewein,	Mr. B. Hague, 1739, 8vo.	Dutch Relation, Dort, 1728, 4to.	

The

a 3

The early difcoveries of the Spaniards in this Ocean, between South
America and Papua, have hitherto
been involved in fuch obfcurity,
that every attempt to explain them
has been fruitlefs; and Geogra-
phers, giving way to their conjec-
tures, have been carried into the
moft egregious contradictions.

Ramufio, Galvano, Herrera, Ba-
ros, De Couto, Lopez Vaz, and
Ovalle, have in this work been
collated to elucidate the early voyages of the Spaniards; but not-
withftanding the affiftance of a
curious Spanifh memorial, and all
the pains which have been taken,
a very imperfect account can be
given

given of the expeditions and difcoveries antecedent to 1595.

There are two relations of Mendana's voyage in 1595. The one
a Spanish manuscript copy of a
letter written by Quiros, at the very
time, to Dr. D. Antonio Morga,
then Lieutenant-General of the
Philipinas, and afterwards, in 1616,
Prefident of the Royal Audience
of Quito, who published it in a
work printed at Mexico in 1609.
The other relation is a Spanish
fragment published by Thevenot,
and added to fome copies of his
collection: but not having the for-
tune to meet fuch a copy of Thevenot's collection, the Author has
been under the necessity to relie

on the tranflation given by Church-
ill in the 5th volume of his collection.   As this voyage of Mendana
is equally curious and important,
the two relations have been collated,
and reduced to one connected de-
tail.   Some Spanifh writers mention a relation of Mendana's voyage in 1595, by Chriftoval Suarez
de Figueroa, in the life of Don
Garcia Hurtado de Mendoça, 4th
Marquis of Canete, then Viceroy
of Peru : perhaps the fragment
preferved by Thevenot is a tran-
fcript of Figueroa.

Quiros, in the conclufion of his
letter to Morga, fays, " The fecret
" being with me, I muft intreat
" you that nobody know it ; it is
" proper

" proper the firft iflands * remain
" concealed till his majefty is in-
" formed, and can give order what
" is expedient for his fervice: for
" as they are in the intermediate
" fpace between Peru, New-Spain
" and the Philipinas, fhould the
" Englifh, on getting an account
" of them, make an eftablifhment
" there, it would be of very bad
" confequence."

Fortunately for the Spaniards the Englifh had not this information at the period when difcoveries were a darling purfuit; for it cannot be doubted Quiros's obfervation, fo well grounded in itfelf, would have been then verified.

* The Marquefas.

Tor-

Torquemada, in his Monarchia Indiana, Vol. I. L. 5. ch. 64. has inserted a relation of Quiros's voyage in 1606. This relation contains many curious and interesting circumstances, but is far from being distinct in the geographical situations. It must also be confessed, that Torquemada's narration is so much interrupted, and his stile so very obscure, that it is not surprizing no one has hitherto made a translation of him; and perhaps, without the assistance of a Spanish memorial, he must have continued unintelligible.

This memorial was presented, to the King of Spain, by Juan Louis Arias. It is contained in a very curious

curious collection of original papers, in two volumes, taken from
the archives of Spain, formerly belonging to M. Colbert's library:
the papers are without order or
connection; some of them manuscripts, some the printed memorials
laid before the Council of the Indies.
Arias's memorial is in print, but
without date: it appears however
to have been presented about 1620.
This memorial contains many circumstances of situation omitted by
Torquemada.

It is much to be regretted, Torquemada has not preserved Quiros's
relation in his very words; but being a pedantick conceited writer, if
we may judge from those pieces of

Quiros

Quiros we have entire, he has much perverted his original.   Don Antonio Ulloa mentions, that Fr. Diego de Cordova, in his Chronica de la Religion Serafica de S. Francisco, L. 1. ch. 21 & 22. has given a circumstantial account of Quiros's voyage in 1606.   It is also said, that Quiros's journals are extant in the library of Barcia; perhaps these may be the papers of which Solorzano speaks in his book De Jure Indiarum, where he relates, that the original papers of Quiros's life were put into his hands by Quiros's son.

The memorial of Quiros, preserved in Spanish by Purchas, is one of the most curious papers
ever

ever written: being ill printed, and not without obſcurities, it has not hitherto been tranſlated: indeed without a ſtrict attention to Torquemada and Arias, it would ſcarce be intelligible. Other elucidations have been thrown into notes. . The Author's own experience and obſervation enabling him to explain and confirm many circumſtances about the pearls, of which Quiros himſelf was doubtful.

There are two relations publiſhed of Roggewein's voyage: one in Dutch at Dort 1728, 4to. republiſhed 1758. The other in French, at the Hague in 1739, two volumes, 8vo. The laſt is a very poor performance, wrote with much

much ignorance, under a parade of knowledge. The Author of the Lives of the Governors of Batavia fays, the original journal, which he had in his poffeffion, is very confonant to the Hague relation; but the only place whofe fituation he mentions, is one degree and a half different in latitude, and double that in longitude from the Hague publication. His affertion therefore means nothing. The Dutch is very different from the French in dates and fituations. It appears the Author of the French relation kept no journal, but writes from memory, and that the Dutch is an abftract of a fea-journal *, to which

* The French relation fays, They arrived at Mocha Ifland on the 10th of March; the Dutch fays on the 15th

which the circumstances of description have been added perhaps from verbal report, with some exaggeration towards the marvelous. The French seems to be faithful in the relation of those things the Author saw, and in many circumstances is confirmed by the Dutch relation.

15th of February : the French says they lay there three days, and the fourth day after their departure saw Juan Fernandes, and got in two days after, which therefore muft have been the 18th or 19th of March. It adds, they staid at Juan Fernandes three weeks, and sailed in March, which is inconsistent with what was before-mentioned. The Dutch relation says, they saw Juan Fernandes on the 24th of February, and continued there from the 25th of February to the 17th of March, which is three weeks, the time the French says they continued there.

A Geo-

A

Geographical Defcription

Iflands and Countries hitherto difcovered in the Southern Part
of the PACIFICK OCEAN, between AMERICA and PAPUA.

THE land neareft America, not to
mention the Iflands of Juan Fernandes, or the Gallapagos, as foreign to the
immediate object of this difcuffion, *an in-
veftigation of difcoveries towards the Continent*, appears to be that country difcovered
by Juan Fernandes, of which Arias fays,

The country was very fertile and agreeable, inhabited by white people, mighty
well difpofed, of our ftature, cloathed with
very fine cloths.

On this coaft Juan Fernandes faw the
mouths of very large rivers, from whence,

B   and

Geographical Description of

and from what the natives intimated, and becaufe the people are fo white, fo well clad, and in every thing elfe fo different from thofe of Chili and Peru, he concluded it certainly the coaft of the Southern Continent, which appeared much better and richer than Peru.

The exact fituation of this difcovery is not diftinctly related, but it appears to be 40° S. 90° W. about 40° S. long. about 90° W.

The next land, which feems to be part of the fame continent, was feen in 1599 by Theodore Gerards (one of the fleet in the voyage wherein W. Adams was pilot) 64° S. who, being carried by tempefts into 64° S. in that height, the country was mountainous and covered with fnow, looking like Norway, and feemed to extend towards the Iflands of Salomon.

The Orange, one of the Naffau fleet, on her arrival at Juan Fernandes 1624, reported, twice on her paffage, to have

5

feen

seen the Southern Continent, once in 50° S. and again in the latitude of 41° S.

Le Maire in 51° S. (or 51° 50′ S. according to Schouten) fell in with some green drift, which he imagined came from land. In 51° 12′ S. Schouten says they had smooth water with the wind at West, and found a tide setting to the northward. In 44° 39′ S. Le Maire saw many birds, being then, by their chart, nearly in the meridian of Juan Fernandes Mas-afuera.

So many concurrent testimonies clearly evince, that the coast of the Southern Continent is but a very little to the westward of the common track towards Juan Fernandes.

It appears, from these intimations, that the East coast of the Continent must lye nearly in a meridional direction; and this is confirmed by Roggewein having signs of land in 28° S. long. 94° 30′ W. which signs continuing, in a course westward for 12°, it is obvious the coast of the Continent runs

　　　　to

to the weftward in about the latitude of
28° S. It appears, from Quiros's track,
that no part of it can run much nearer the
equator before the meridian of 160° W.
longitude. In about 147° long. in 26° S.
he had figns of the Continent: and at
Sagittaria, in 17° 40' S. long. 158° W. he
had intimations of large countries in that
neighbourhood; and Le Maire about 160°
W. long. obferves, the great fwell from the
South, which they had for fome days before, then ceafed; fo that probably about
the long. 165° W. is the northernmoft point
of the Continent.

In the year 1687 Wafer mentions, that
Captain Davis, with whom Dampier went
into the South Sea, failing from the Gallapagos towards Juan Fernandes, in 27° 20' S.
fell in with a fmall low fandy Ifland without any rocks around it. To the weftward,
about 12 leagues (36') by judgement, they
faw a range of high land which they took
to be Iflands, for there were feveral partitions in the profpect. This land feemed to
reach

reach about 14 or 16 leagues in a range, and there came from thence great flocks of fowls. Wafer fays, the fmall Ifland bears from Copiapo, almoft due W. 500 leagues (1500′) and from the Gallapagos under the line 600 leagues (1800′). Wafer does not feem to have kept a journal, and the two pofitions are inconfiftent, for 600 leagues, from even the moft eaftern of the Galla-pagos, would in the lat. of 27° 20′ S. be more than 500 leagues from Copiapo. As they came from the Gallapagos that diftance appears the moft to be relied on, for the other can only be conjecture; and there appears greater probability that the reckon-ing fhould be correct from the Gallapagos to Sandy Ifland, than from Sandy Ifland to Juan Fernandes. Accordingly, by Thorn-ton's map, publifhed not many years after this difcovery, Sandy Ifland is placed in 27° 20′ S. 106° W.

27° 20′ S.
106° W.

From whence it appears, the land dif-covered by Davis was the Ifland fince named Eafter by the Dutch.

B 3   This

Lat. & Long.
from London.
27° S.
106° 30′ W.

This Island was defcried by them 6th April 1722. It is 16 leagues (48′) in circuit. 8th, They entered a gulph to the S. E. and anchored there. The country is all planted, fown and till'd; the fquares are feparated from each other with much exactnefs, and the limits formed by line. It is full of woods and forefts, and there are fome elevated places fit for the culture of vines. Almoft all the fruits and plants were now at maturity; the fields and trees were abundantly loaded.

It is very full of people, they are in general brown like Spaniards, fome were blackifh, and others quite white, and others of which the complexion is reddifh as if burnt by the fun. Their ears hang down to their fhoulders, and fome few wore in them two white balls, as a mark of great ornament; their bodies were painted with all kinds of figures of birds and other animals, fome much handfomer than others: their women were in general painted with rouge extreamly lively, and which much furpaffes any thing the

Dutch

Dutch knew. They could not difcover of what thefe Iflanders compofe a colour fo fine. They cover themfelves with red and white coverlits, and wear a fmall hat made of rufhes or ftraw. The ftuff of which the coverlits were made was foft to the touch like filk, and it feemed they had the materials for manufacturing it.

The inhabitants of this Ifland have no arms, but truft entirely to their idols, erected in numbers on the coaft. Thefe ftatues were all of ftone, of the figure of a man with great ears. The head was adorned with a crown; the whole executed and proportioned according to the rules of art, which aftonifhed the Dutch much; about thefe idols at 20 or 30 paces round there was an enclofure made of white ftones *.

Several

* The Dutch relation fays, " Every perfon wore " cloaths, which were of different colours and hand- " fome, ftitched or woven of filk and cotton. Their " ears are horribly long, and in moft of them hung " upon their fhoulders; they had large holes in them " that we could eafily put our hands through. The " men had their bodies painted with a red or dark

" brown,

Several of the inhabitants attended the idols more frequently and with more devout zeal, whence they were concluded to be priefts: it was alfo obferved they had fome marks of diftinction, as great balls hanging at their ears, and their heads fhaved; they wore a bonnet made of black and white feathers, exactly refembling thofe of a ftork. There was one came aboard who was quite white; he had pendants in his ears round and

" brown, and the women with a fcarlet colour."
This account defcribes them to be giants. It fays,
" After the natives had fuffered by our weapons,
" they brought us from their hutts all kinds of the
" fruits of the country, fugar-canes with jambe-
" jambes, plantains, and a great quantity of fowls.

" Two ftones, of a fize almoft beyond belief,
" ferved them for gods: the one was broad above
" meafure, and lay upon the ground; upon this
" ftood the other ftone, which was very high, and
" of fuch extent that feven of our people, with out-
" ftretched arms, would hardly have been able to
" have encircled it, and it was full as high as three
" men. Towards the top of the ftone was cut or
" carved the figure of a man's head adorned with a
" garland, which was in mofaic or inlaid-work, not
" ill perform'd.

" The

and white, of the fize of a fift; he had an air extreamly devout.

In the morning the natives were observed proftrate towards the rifing Sun, and that they had lighted many fires as burntofferings to their idols.

The natives appeared to be under the government of the oldeft, for it was obfervable in each houfe or family the moft antient governed and gave orders: the moft

" The name of the largeft ftone idol was Taurico, " and of the other Dago; at leaft thefe were the " words they called to them by, and wherewith they " worfhipped them.

" The favages had great refpect for thefe two idols " Taurico and Dago, and approached them with " great reverence, dancing, fhouting, jumping, and " clapping their hands. When the cannon, of " which they feemed to be in great apprehenfion, " were difcharged, and the fhot founded in their " ears, they made furprizing and wonderful geftures " and leaps, and pointed with their fingers, firft to " our people and then to their gods, whom they ap- " peared to fupplicate for help againft us, and to call " upon with a frightful fhout and howling of Dago, " Dago."

aged

Lat. & Long. from London.
27° S.
106° 30′ W.

aged amongſt them had on their heads plumes reſembling thoſe of the Oſtrich, and a ſtick in their hands. The Dutch were driven off by a weſterly wind, and kept driving about for ſome days in the ſame latitude, and then bore away towards Schouten's diſcoveries, and, by ſtanding W. N. W. ſaw no more birds.

S. 15°12′ ⎫
L. 15°13′ ⎬ S.
140° 31′ W. ⎭

Dog Iſland was diſcovered 10th April 1616. It is a very low ſmall Iſland without ſoundings, except cloſe in ſhore, where the boat found 25 fathom, a ſhort muſket-ſhot from ſhore, and ſo great a ſurf that it could not land ; the people ſwam aſhore ; they found no freſh water, but ſome ponds of rain-water which was very bitter. The Iſland is formed around by a border covered with fine trees, but within, in many places, it was filled with ſalt water. This Iſland has plenty of water-creſſes which are very bitter to the taſte, pungent, purgative, and good for the ſcurvy. There is here plenty of ſnakes and fiſh near the Iſland, and aſhore many

many Gulls and other birds roosting on the trees.

Le Maire's journal says, it is the Island Magellan, called Desventurada, of which Jerome Benzon wrote them, that it was three leagues in circuit, so low in some places that the sea flows into the middle of the Island with the tide. The Dutch saw on it three Spanish dogs very lean.

This day they had the wind N. and the night after their departure it blew very hard with much rain.

Las Marquesas, discovered by Alvaro Mendana de Neyra, 21st July 1595, are four in number, La Magdalena, S. Pedro, Dominica, and S. Christina.

La Magdalena has a port on the south side of the Island, in 10° S. They passed on the south side of Magdalena, it is high and steep to the sea, mountainous with vallies where the Indians dwell. It is about

six

six leagues (21′) in circuit, and appears to be very populous, as 70 veffels came out from the port on the fouth-fide of the Ifland with above 400 Indians, fome on Cattamarans, others fwimming; they were white and of a gentle difpofition, large ftout limbed, and fo well fhaped as greatly to furpafs the Spaniards; they had beautiful teeth, eyes and mouth, delicate fine hands and feet, flowing hair, and many of them with it very fair; and amongft them were fome moft beautiful boys, all of them naked and without covering to any part, and all of their bodies, legs and arms, and fome with their faces, painted in the manner of the Biffayas, that is by punctuation. Being invited aboard, about 40 came, and amongft them one taller than any of the Spaniards. They were great thieves, and the Spaniards lofing patience fired to frighten them, whereupon they all leaped into the water, and put themfelves on their defence; and founding a fhell fome difcharged ftones from flings, others threatened with their lances; one of

the

the ftones, after it had ftruck the fhip's fide,

wounded a foldier; five or fix of the

Indians were killed from the fhip; after-

wards three came out in a canoe, one had

a green bough, and fomething white in

his hand, and brought off cocoa-nuts.

Lat. & Long.
from London.
10° S.
143° 42′ W.

N.W. 10 leagues (34′) from Magdalena
lies S. Pedro, it is 3 leagues (10′) in circuit; it is an ifland of good profpect, having
much wood and fine plains, very level and
not high; they could not tell if it was inhabited as they did not approach it.

To the N.W. of S. Pedro, about 5 leagues
(17′) is La Dominica; it is of a very beautiful appearance, and feemed very populous.
It is about 15 leagues (51′) in circuit; it
ftretches N. E. and S.W. It appeared pleafant, having fine plains and hills, on which
were tokens of much wood.

Several canoes of Indians came out, fome
darker coloured than others, amongft them

5   a

a comely old man who had a green bough and something white in one hand.

An Indian came on board who with much ease lifted up a calf by the ear. Four handsome Indians having got aboard one of them, snatched up a curious bitch, and giving a shout they all boldly leaped with her into the sea, and swam away to their canoes.

To the southward of La Dominica, little more than 1 league ($3\frac{1}{2}′$) is another Island, about 8 or 9 leagues (27 or 31′) in circuit, called S. Christina, thro' the channel between them the squadron passed, it is clear, as are all parts they saw of these Islands.

On the west side of S. Christina in 9° 30′ S. is the port named Madre de Dios, sheltered from all winds; it is shaped like a horse-shoe, the neck or entrance very narrow; at the mouth there is 30 fathom, 24 in the middle of the harbour, and 12 close to the shore.

The

The ifland is well peopled, it is fome-what high, has vallies and hollows where the Indians dwell.

Lat. & Long. from London. 10° S. 143° 42´ W.

There appears out at fea five fmall groves facing the harbour, and a ridge of hills, which divides two ftrands, with a fpring of excellent water, which falls from a fmall height, and near it a brook, as good as it, running clofe to a little town of the Indians, fo that the fpring, brook, and town, are together by the fhore at the foot of the hill on the north fide. On the fouth fide are fome houfes among trees, and on the eaft fome rocks and cliffs, whence the brook flows. This harbour is known by a rock on the fouth fide next the fea, and on the north fide a hollow.

The town is like two fides of a fquare, one north and fouth, the other eaft and weft, with the avenues well paved; the reft like an open place encompaffed with thick trees, which from the defcription ap-pear to be the rima or bread fruit.

Their

Their houfes are built like double galle-
ries, the floor higher than the ftreet, abundance of people feemed to live in each of
them, becaufe there were many beds; fome
had low doors, others had all the front
open; they are made of timber interwoven
with bamboe.

When the Spaniards landed, they marched
round the town, the Indians not offering to
ftir; they then halted and called to them,
when about 300 came: the Spaniards drew
a line on the ground, making figns that they
muft not pafs it, and afking water; the
Indians brought it in cocoa-nuts, with fome
fruit.

The Indians in the Ifland did not feem
fo white as thofe of Magdalena. The women
came out and made no difficulty of fetting
down by the Spaniards. The Spaniards
affirmed the women have moft beautiful
faces, delicate hands, a good fhape, and
flender waift; many of them far exceeding
the moft accomplifhed women of Lima,
                                        they

they were white, but not ruddy; they were clad from the breaſt downward with a ſort of tunicks, curiouſly wove of delicate fine palm-tree-leaves.

Lat. & Long,
from London.
10° S.
143° 42′ W.

The conſtitution, health and corpulency of theſe people ſhew the goodneſs of the air they live in, cloaths could well be born with day or night, the ſun was not very troubleſome, ſome great rains fell; there was never any dew but a dry air, inſomuch that whatever was left on the ground wet over-night was dry in the morning, without being hung and laid out; but it is not known if it be ſo all the year.

Without the town they had ſome pira-guas long and handſomely wrought out of one piece of wood with a ſort of keel, head and ſtern raiſed with boards faſt bound with ropes made of the cocoa; each of them will carry between 30 and 40 men to row: being aſked to what uſe they put them, they gave to underſtand they went in them to other parts; they work them

C   with

with little hatchets made of fish bones and shells, and sharpen them on great stones for the purpose.

The Indians seeing a negro with the Spaniards, made signs toward the south, that there were such, and that they went there in their great canoes to fight, and that the others had arrows.

The refreshments found here were hogs and fowls like those in Spain, sugar-canes, very fine plantains, cocoa-nuts, the bread-fruit, a fruit like chesnuts inclosed in prickles, it resembles the chesnut in taste, but is bigger than six chesnuts, many of them were roasted and boiled; nuts about the bigness and much like walnuts in taste, their shell is very hard and all of a piece without any joining, the kernell is not interwoven with the shell, but so loose that when cracked it drops out whole; they eat and carried away a great many; they are very oily, and many who eat them suspected they occasioned fluxes. They also saw
Spanish

Spanish pumpkins sowed on the shore, and amongst them some flowers beautiful to the eye but without smell.

At a distance from the town was an oracle or place of worship palisaded about; the entrance on the west side; almost in the middle of it stood a house with a door to the north, in which were some mishapen wooden figures, and some eatable things offered there; amongst the rest a hog, which the Spanish soldiers took down, and being about to take away other things, the Indians hindered them, making signs that they should not touch them, and shewing that they had a respect for that house and figures.

The Spaniards landed with their wives, 28th July, to hear mass said, at which the Indians present were very silent and attentive, kneeling and quietly doing all they saw the Spaniards do. A beautiful Indian woman sat down near Dᵃ. Ysabella, Mendana's wife, to fan her, and she seeing the

Indian's

Indian's hair so very fair, endeavoured to have some of it cut off; but seeing she avoided it they forbore for fear of angering her.

The Adelentado returning aboard, disputes arose, and many of the Indians were killed. In the opinion of the Spanish author, the Spaniards were aggressors.

The arms, language and embarkations of this Island were the same as those of Magdalena.

The next Island, named La Encarnacion, was discovered by Quiros, 26th January 1606. It is a small Island about 4 leagues (14′) in circuit, low and level with the water, with few trees, the greater part being sandy; it had no soundings or port.

They sailed two days to the westward, having some rain; and next day, at break of day, were near another Island, having the evening before seen many birds. They

run

run along the fouth-fide, and eftimated it might be 12 leagues (41′). It was plain and even at top, without foundings; for tho' the Zabra anchored almoft in the furf, in 10 fathom, they had no ground 200 a-ftern; it was called S. Juan Baptifta. It appears to be the Ifland of which Arrias fays, when Quiros arrived at the latitude of 26° S. he faw to the fouthward very large hanging clouds and a very thick horizon, with other known figns of a Continent, and a little Ifland inhabited by various kinds of birds of very fweet notes which never breed in nor vifit places but a little diftance from main land.

Lat. & Long.
from London.
25° S.
146° 9′ W.

It appears obvious, the latter longitudes, in the French relation of Róggewein's voyage, are very erroneous : the fituations given in the Dutch are therefore adopted. Perhaps fome of the Iflands feen by Roggewein are the fame feen by Schouten, tho' it appears more probable the Iflands at which Roggewein loft one fhip, and thofe adjoining, lie between Dog Ifland and Son-

dre-

dre-Grond of Schouten; and as such are here described.

The first Island Roggewein saw, after leaving Easter Island, was, by some, imagined to be the same Schouten named Dog Island; others thought it a new discovery, and named it Carlshoff. The Dutch relation makes no mention of it; but the French describes it to be very low, with a kind of lake in the middle, with yellowish sand on the shore. It is about 3 leagues (9′) in circuit.

15° 45′ S.
139° 30′ W.

The S. E. trade began here to change, and veer about to the S. W. and carried them unexpectedly next night amongst several Islands.

14° 41′ S.
140° 6′ W.

These Islands are four in number, each 4 or 5 leagues (12 or 15′) in compass. One of the ships got in amongst some rocks where she was lost, tho' the people were saved. These Islands are environ'd with rocks; that where the ship was lost,

4   was

was named Pernicious Ifland; two others, The Brothers; and the fourth, The Sifter. They were all four adorned with a delightful verdure, and furnifhed with fine trees, amongft which were plenty of cocoa-nuts: there was alfo plenty of herbs, which were extremely beneficial to the fick: plenty of mufcles, of *nacres*, mother of pearl, and pearl oyfters, were found here; fo that there is great profpect of an advantageous pearl fifhery; befides, fome pearls were found in oyfters, which the natives had torn from the rocks. Thefe Iflands are extremely low, fo that fome places were then overflowed. The natives navigate in good canoes, and other veffels, provided with cables and fails. The inhabitants of the Ifland, where the fhip was loft, are larger than thofe of Eafter Ifland; they had their bodies painted of all colours; their hair very long, in colour black, and brown inclining a little to red; they carry pikes from 18 to 20 feet long; their countenances do not indicate a difpofition gentle or humane; they are very cruel and vicious: they endea-

C 4   voured

voured to draw the Dutch into an ambuſ-
cade to attack them with advantage, in revenge for their firing upon thoſe who came
down to the ſhore when the ſhip was loſt.
They keep in companies of 50 or 100 men.
The coaſt has bad ſoundings: they were
detained five days before they got clear of
theſe Iſlands*.

* The Dutch relation ſays, " 20th May, We
" came into 14° 41′ S. where we fell in with a great
" number of ſunken rocks, rocks above water, and
" ſmall Iſlands, all cloſe together; ſo that we were
" of opinion they had been joined formerly and made
" one land, but ſeparated afterwards by the ſea.
 " Amongſt theſe the moſt conſiderable was broken
" with many waters and ſtreams. In this labyrinth
" of Iſlands and rocks we had the woeful misfortune
" to loſe one ſhip, which ſtruck upon the rocks and
" beat to pieces. It was impoſſible for the ſhips to
" approach very near the land, on account of the
" high breakers on the ſhore. There is no anchoring
" ground; it is a low, ſandy, rocky Iſland, being
" almoſt all overflowed within ; but on the borders
" it is full of trees, tho' amongſt them neither pal-
" metos nor cocoa-nuts were to be found, which is
" probably the reaſon it is uninhabited."
It is probable theſe two deſcriptions, ſo very diſſo-
nant, relate to different Iſlands in the ſame cluſter.

The

The day after they left them, they saw an Island, which was named Aurora, because it was discovered at day-break. It is about 4 leagues (12′) in circuit; it is covered with bushes and trees, and adorned with a very beautiful verdure. There was no fit anchorage.

Towards evening they saw another, which they named Vesper. It is about 12 leagues (36′) in circuit; very low, otherwise extremely beautiful, and covered with trees †.

Keeping a course always to the westward, next day they discovered more land, and saw here and there smoaks; and approaching the land perceived many inhabitants

---

† The Dutch relation takes no notice of Aurora or Vesper: it says, " 25th May, We passed by the " Island of Flies, discovered by Schouten. The in- " land parts of it are likewise full of salt water, and " it has plenty of wild green trees. It is inhabited " by savages of a large stature, armed with bows and arrows.

143° 52′ W.

" The Island swarms with nasty flies, which were very troublesome for two or three days."

passing

paffing along fhore. They afterwards found it was an affemblage of Iflands quite clofe together. They were fix in number, all very pleafant, and taken together might be 30 leagues (90′) in extent. They were named Labyrinth, as the Dutch were obliged to make many turnings before they got clear of thefe Iflands‡.

Some days after they difcovered another Ifland of a good height, and beautiful. This Ifland was named Recreation. It is about 12 leagues (36′) in circuit. The land is very fertile, it has many trees, particularly palms, cocoa-nuts, and iron wood. The Iflanders were of a moderate height, ftrong and robuft, lively and well made ; their hair long, black and fhining, being anointed with cocoa-nut oil ; they had all their bodies painted as thofe of Eafter

‡ The Dutch relation fays, " 29th May, We " paffed among a number of rocks and iflands, from " whence we fometimes faw a fmoak afcend, a fign " that they were inhabited ; but we had no oppor- " tunity of going afhore."

Ifland.

Ifland*. The men cover their middle with a net, which paffes between their thighs; but the women were entirely covered with a ftuff as foft to the touch as filk. They alfo had ornaments of mother of pearl around their bodies and arms. As there was not much fhelter for the fhips, and the ground bad for anchoring, they made no ftay: the high cliffs prevented all fight

---

* The Dutch relation fays, " 1ft of June, We " came in fight of an Ifland hitherto unknown to " Europeans: thither we went in our boats in order " to take a view of it, and to procure refrefhments; " when the inhabitants, who faw us approach from " afar, came down to the fhore to make us return " back, and to prevent our landing.

" Thefe people were of an excellent carriage, " well made and very beautiful, and their fkins as " clear and white as that of a native of Holland.

" As foon as we came near they jumped like mad- " men into the water to meet us, and pufhed with " great fiercenefs with their weapons, which were " fpears and lances, whofe points were arm'd with a " very fharp wood as hard as iron; whereupon we " fired our mufquets, which made them take to their " heels; they fled to a high fteep rock, which they " fcrambled up like monkies, with incredible agility. " From thence, being convinced of our fuperior " force,

Lat. & Long.
from London.
15° 47′ S.
147° 30′ W.

fight of the interior country. The Dutch having fired upon the natives, were drawn into an ambufcade, and obliged to retreat with the lofs of feveral men.

The next Ifland difcovered by Le Maire, 14th April 1616, was named Sondre-

S. 15° 15′ } S.
L. 14° 35′ }
147° 47′ W.

Grond, as having no foundings, or change in the colour of the water, at a fhort mufquet fhot off fhore. They faw plenty of

" force, they gave us to underftand hoftilities fhould
" ceafe. Being in the utmoft want of all manner of
" refrefhments, we did every thing to allure them to
" us. They brought us their commodities, confift-
" ing of cocoa-nuts and a bitter herb, tafting like
" Dutch creffes, which is found here in great plenty;
" for thofe we gave them in exchange fmall looking-
" glaffes, glafs beads of all colours, combs, bells,
" and a number of fuch toys of little value, where-
" with they were extremely pleafed."

The Indians afterwards decoyed and attacked them in a narrow path, hurling down ftones upon them.

" Thefe people are well-proportioned, and wear,
" as an ornament, pearls of a large fize in their ears.
" About their necks and bodies they wear, as a fin-
" gular ornament, the fhells of pearl oyfters. We
" received great relief in the fcurvy from the bitter
" herb, which is found here in great plenty."

birds

birds and fish. The Island is low, having many trees here and there. They failed S. and S. S.W. to get round the Island; and having run in the night about 10 leagues (40′) S. S.W. in the morning, they stood in shore.

This Island is not broad though long : it extends nearest N. E. and S. W. and might be about 20 leagues (80′) in circuit. It is very low, and had, on the outside, a bank like a wall, furnished with palmetos and cocoa-nut trees, but within full of falt water.

About a league from shore a canoe came off with four men, quite naked, of a red colour, having hair long and black ; they would not come aboard, but kept a good distance off, crying with a loud voice, and making signs to the Dutch to come to the shore. The Dutch saw people adjoining to the wood, setting near the shore, who were of complexion very yellow, inclining

to

to red, with long hair, extremely black, tucked up behind.

When the Dutch ftood in again towards the fhore, the Indians fometimes fhewing their veftments, fometimes branches of trees, made figns to come afhore. The boat being fent to found, a canoe with three men came to it; the people were prefented with three knives and fome beads, which feemed very agreeable to them. They gave their left hand in fign of friendfhip, but would not go to the fhip: they feemed ravifhed in admiration at feeing fo great a veffel, fo high, and with fo many and fo great fails: they were very defirous of iron. They have hair quite black, which they tie on the head or on the fhoulders. They are yellow and brown in complexion, and have their fkins, particularly their fingers, marked with many figures, long, round and fquare, according to Le Maire; but according to Schouten they are marked with various figures, as ferpents, dragons, and fuch like;
and

and it looked as if they had been burnt with gun-powder. The Indians intimating they were well provided with hogs and fowls, the boat was sent ashore with some few things to truck with them; but as soon as the Dutch got ashore, about thirty men sallied out of the wood, carrying large wooden clubs, and seized two men, whom they pulled out of the boat, with an intention of carrying them into the wood; but being fired at, they left the two men and fled into the wood. These Indians had large long staffs, having things at the end resembling the swords or horns of fish; they also use slings.

Leaving this Island they had no swell, as the preceding days; from whence it was presumed, that towards the South there was more land or some Islands.

Waterland was discovered by Le Maire, 16th April 1616. It was found destitute of soundings to anchor; it was low, sandy and full of rocks, being within quite covered with

Lat. & Long. from London.
S. 15°15' ⎱
L. 14°35' ⎰ S.
147° 47' W.

14° 45' S.
148° 33' W.

with falt water; but on the border full of trees, not cocoa-nuts or palmetos, but another kind unknown. The boat anchoring in 40 fathom very bad ground, fome of the people got afhore, and found, a little way from the fhore, fome ditches with frefh water, alfo a few garden-creffes and Indian fallad: the water was tranfported in fmall barrels to the fhore; but it was very inconvenient to get it aboard, for the boat could not come to the fhore, as there was a great furf againft the ftrand; but lay at anchor fo far off that the people were obliged to fwim and haul one another afhore with ropes, fo that it was with great trouble they got off four cafks of water. They alfo found herbs, like thofe at Dog Ifland, tafting like creffes, of which was made a pottage which gave great relief to the fick: they alfo found here fome lobfters, cockles, and periwinkles.

They ftood from hence W. S. W. to get into 15° S. or more, not to pafs the bay of Quiros, having the wind at Eaft, tho' faint

during

during the day, with rain and fmooth water;
they were in 14° 46′ S.

17th. Had a good fhower; this day faw many kinds of birds, having very large wings, which evinced that there was land to the South.

18th. Difcovered another low Ifland,
ftretching W. N. W. and E. S. E. as long as could be feen; approaching it the boat was fent to found, and found ground about a mufket-fhot from fhore, on a rocky fpit, at 20, 25 and 40 fathom, the depths very irregular. The fkiff was fent with two empty cafks, when it was near the fhore the people left it at anchor and fwam afhore; they went into the wood to look for water, but as they faw a large-bodied favage with a bow in his hand, as if to fhoot fifh, they immediately retired to the fkiff, and returned aboard; when they were at a little diftance from the ftrand, five or fix naked favages came upon the fhore; but feeing our people were gone off, they returned to the wood.

D   In

In this Island there is great plenty of fine forest trees, but within it is also overflowed with salt water. There were so many flies that no part of the boat which was out of the water was to be seen for them; this plague lasted for three days, and would have continued much longer if a fresh wind had not sprung up. This day the weather was fine, and the water smooth. This Island was named Fly Island.

After they left this Island, they stood to the Westward, making little sail in the night, and sometimes lying-to: the two following days it rained much.

22d. The wind was N. the weather bad, with much thunder and lightning to the S.

S. 15°4′ } S.
L. 15°50′ }

23d. The wind was sometimes from N.E. but chiefly from E. and E. by S. they had again a large swell from the South, which continued the following days, it was from thence concluded there was no land to the S. or at least that it was very far distant *.

* It is obvious from Quiros, that there is no main land for 800 miles to the Southward in this longitude.

24th.

24th. Wind E. there fell fome heavy fhowers of rain, they alfo faw many birds.

25th. Saved four cafks of rain-water.

28th. They had the wind at E. the courfe 15° $10'$ S. W. by S. in the night it was calm.

1ft May. The wind E. it rained very hard; the fwell from the South began to abate.

3d. The wind E. S. E. faw fome Dol- S.15° $3'$ } S. phins, which were the firft they had met L. 15° with in the South-Sea; almoft all their 165° $25'$ W. people had by this time recovered of the fcurvy, by the affiftance of the plants they had found at Dog Ifland and Waterland.

8th. They perceived they approached the land by fome branches of trees floating in the fea.

9th. Afternoon, faw a fail ftanding to 15° $20'$ S. the North, and coming from the South.' 182° $7'$ W.

D 2   Having

Having continued Schouten and Le
Maire's track, from Fly Island to a known
point, it is neceffary to return back to the
other Iflands difcovered by Quiros. What
has been mentioned, from Schouten and Le
Maire, will be ufeful in confirming the reports received by Quiros from the natives of
one of thefe Iflands, that there were large
countries in the neighbourhood.

28° S.

' Santelmo, difcovered 4th February 1606,
was fo named from a corpo fanto having
fettled on the maft the night before, the
weather having then been fqually and dirty.
They found this Ifland to be 30 leagues
(103') in circuit, overflown in the middle,
and furrounded with a reef of rocks, appearing to be coral; though they fought
carefully they got no port or foundings *.

Next day they left four other Iflands,
like to it in every other refpect; they were
named Quatro Coronadas.

* This Ifland *muft* have been *long*, as Quiros could
not otherwife have, in fo fhort a time, examined it
carefully for a port.

And

Lat. & Long.
from London.

And paſſed on to the W. N. W. toward another Iſland, which appeared to be about 10 leagues (34') in circuit; it ſtretches from N. to S. and was like the others; it was named S. Miguel Archangel.

Another to the W. N. W. was named La Convercion de S. Paulo; it was of the ſame kind.

9th February 1606, at day-break, they had ſight of an Iſland to the North. They paſſed on, leaving it to windward, being in 18° 40' S. It was named La Dezena, or the Tenth Iſland *.

18° 40' S.

The 10th, they diſcovered an Iſland and columns of ſmoak ariſing in ſeveral places. The Zabra was ſent in ſhore, and anchored in 10 fathom foul ground; they ſaw on the beach about 100 Indians, who joyfully made ſigns to them; but the ſurf beat againſt the

17° 40' S.

* It muſt lie nearly in the ſame meridian as San-telmo, as the difference of latitude (560') is as much as they can be ſuppoſed to have run in five days.

rocks

rocks with great violence, and deterred them from landing; at length one of the Spaniards leaped into the sea, and getting to the rocks scrambled up one of them; the Indians, pleased with his resolution, went out to receive him, embracing him with much shew of affection, and often kissing his forehead. The Spaniard doing the like, to repay their good will and caresses. Some other Spaniards, following this example, were received in like manner by the Indians. These valiant savages carried in their hands large wooden lances, burnt at the ends, from 25 to 30 palms long; others swords of palmwood, and others great clubs. They dwell in thatched-houses on the brink of the sea, amongst the palms, whereof there is great abundance; their fruit, and some fish from the sea, serving them for food. They go naked, are in colour Mulattoes, but well limbed, and of good carriage. The Spaniards treated with them by signs, and endeavoured to prevail on some to come to the ships, whence they should be sent back cloathed and loaded with presents. Finding the In-

4   dians

dians were not to be prevailed upon, they
returned to the boats; this being perceived
by the Indians, eight or nine of them threw
themfelves into the water, and, with fome
dread, though encouraged by the Spaniards,
came to the boats, who feeing them coming,
ftaid for them, endeavouring to perfuade
them to come aboard, by giving them knives
and other things, with which they feemed
pleafed, but did not chufe to venture aboard,
they returned afhore, where their companions waited for them.

Night approaching, and no probability of
getting the Indians aboard, the boats returned to the fhips, which kept in the offing
all night. When morning came, they found
themfelves about 8 leagues (27′) from that
place, down the coaft: this gave great difguft
to all, as it was impoffible to return back,
or fee the Indians; but difcovering the land
abreaft to be the fame they had left, it was
great fatisfaction to every one, as they knew
it was inhabited.

The

The ſhips kept working to windward for want of a port, and the boat was ſent to look for water and people ; the landing was extreamly difficult and hazardous; but, with much trouble, they dragged the boat over the rocks, the top whereof appeared with the reflux of the waves.

Having got to a little wood of palms and other trees, which was near the ſhore, they were heſitating where they ſhould enter in queſt of water and a town; when, looking to the ſea, they perceived their other boat; they waited for them, and when they were got aſhore, they ſet out together on their way, paſſing thro' the thick wood, ſome of them cutting away the branches with their ſwords, till near another bay of dead water on the other ſide of the Iſland.

Within this wood they diſcovered a round place ſurrounded with ſmall ſtones, and in one part of it were ſome larger, which were raiſed from the ground about a cubit and a half, leaning on a large high tree, from whoſe whofe trunk hung many woven palm-leaves, which fell upon the ftones raifed in form of an altar.

Leaving this, they went to the plain, in queft of water; and feeing another fmall wood oppofite to them, they went into it, where in a fmall meadow, as it was moift and verdant, they dug to find water; but their pains were to little purpofe, for what iffued was brackifh; they prefently alleviated their thirft, for fome climbing up the palms which were there, they cut down plenty of of cocoa-nuts; and, as they could not find water, loaded with them, and walked towards the fhore, with the water to their knee, about half a league; for the force of the fea breaking upon the rocks, extends it along the fhore to the fkirts of the little mountains, joining at high-water, the fea on the other fide of the Ifland, by a fhallow fandy channel between the two little woods. When they arrived at the boats, they found the people left with them had difcovered a narrow gut, by which they entered, without rifk,

rifk, fo near to the fhore, that they were enabled to embark without wetting a foot.

Some of the people, who were left behind, perceived, between the trees, a perfon walking leifurely, going up they found it to be a woman, but fo old in appearance, that it was amazing fhe could ftand on her feet: She appeared to have been in her youth comely, and of a graceful mein; the features of her face, altho' wrinkled and dried up, gave tokens of no little beauty: they told her, by figns, that fhe muft go with them to the fhips; the Indian, without fhewing any uneafinefs or regret, obeyed, going with them to the boat, and in it to the Capitana. The Captain ordered the Indian to be clad, to have meat and drink, and to be carried afhore again, to let the natives know, nothing was meant but peace and friendfhip with them.

When they reached the fhore again, they walked with her along the beach to another oppofite,

oppofite, for fhe directed them thither, point-
ing with her finger, that there were her
people. The Spaniards looking that way,
faw five or fix piraguas drying their fails,
which appeared to be Latine, made of palms,
and they of white wood, well wrought, narrow and long, their feams were joined with
ftrong thongs of the palm, of which tree they
make their cables, fails, and all kinds of arms
and cloathing, wherewith the women adorn
themfelves, from the waift downwards.
They alfo afford them meat and water; and
the Spaniards underftood that it is this alone
they drink, for they could find none in more
than two leagues of the land over which
they went.

The Spaniards being got to the beach,
the Indians took down their fails in great
hafte; and, leaving their veffels at anchor,
landed and came up towards the Spaniards,
who alfo advanced to them. As foon as
they faw the Indian woman, they ran to
embrace her, wondering to fee her cloathed,
embracing alfo the Spaniards with fhew of
affection,

affection, whereupon the Serjeant Pedro Garcia ftept forth, afking, by figns, which of them was chief; he was fhewn a robuft man, of a graceful mein, lively, well-built, and ftrong limbed, with broad cheft and fhoulders, he had on his head a kind of crown made of fmall black feathers, but fo fine and foft that they looked like filk, there fell down backwards a bunch of red hair, fomewhat curled, the ends of which reached to the middle of his back : it caufed in the Spaniards much admiration to fee, amongft thefe Indians who are not white, hair fo perfectly red, altho' they concluded it was of his wife. They made figns for him to go aboard, where he would have prefents made him ; he feemed well pleafed, and, accompanied by his people, went with the Spaniards to the beach, who embarking in the boat, he did the like with fome other Indians; but fcarce were they embarked, when, afraid of fome treachery, they leaped into the water and fled to the fhore. Their chief wanted to do the fame, but was held faft, the boat rowing as faft as they could to

get

get off fhore; they prefently got to the fhip, but all their endeavours to perfuade him to go aboard were to no effect, which the Captain perceiving, he ordered them to cloath him there, giving him food, and affuring him of their good intentions; and, in confirmation thereof, returned him cloathed and free to the fhore. His fpeedy return was of no little importance, for the Indians afhore, who were more than 100, feeing their chief carried prifoner, furrounded three or four Spaniards who remained behind, and threatned them with lances and great clubs. This being obferved from the boats, four or five leaped afhore, and went as faft as they could to join their friends; who, with undaunted refolution, faced the Indians with their mufkets prefented.

At this inftant the Indian chief landed, whereupon the natives were appeafed; and, leaving the Spaniards, went to receive their lord, who with tears of joy, advanced to embrace them, informing them of the good treatment he had received, telling them alfo,

5   that

that the Spaniards were friends, and came in peace.

The Spaniards, by way of festivity, on learning from them, that in their rout were large countries, fired their muskets into the air.

At length, the Indians being embarked, their chief came to our people, and embracing the Serjeant with much affection, took off the crown from his head, and gave it him; expressing, by signs, that he had nothing of greater estimation: he then went aboard his piragua, and setting sail, navigated towards a small islot; and the Spaniards returned to the boats, in which they went on board the ships; they kept working in the offing all night, and next day ran along shore to the N.W. observing the sun in it in 17° 40′ S.'

It seems to be this Island of which Arrias says, " That Quiros, in other Islands, dif-
" covered in the same voyage long before
" that

" that of Taumaco, faw fome boys as fair
" and ruddy as the Flemings, amongft the
" natives of the Iflands, who were of a
" wheat-colour*; and that they intimated
" by figns, that they brought thefe whites
" from a higher latitude to the South."
Thefe Iflands muft have been Sagittaria, becaufe thefe and Ifla de Gente-hermofa (Ifland
of beautiful people) were the only inhabited
Iflands Quiros vifited before Taumaco; and
probably to this are we to refer Torquemada's report, that they had here intimation of
large countries.

‘ Quiros leaving Sagittaria, failed till 14th
February, when they faw an Ifland to the
N. E. they ftood for it; but, being much to
leeward, could not reach it. This Ifland
was named La Fugitiva.

Next day they faw another to the N. E.
which they named La del Peregrina; but
the winds did not admit them to reach it.

* Trigueno.

The

The 21ſt, they deſcried S. Bernardo.'

This Iſland, or Iſlands, was diſcovered in Mendana's voyage 1595. In the firſt voyage they are deſcribed to be four Iſlands cloſe to one another: in this voyage it is called one Iſland; and is deſcribed to have a large lake of ſalt water in the middle; whether it be divided into four Iſlands by narrow channels, or joined together by ſand banks, ſo as to appear four, tho' in fact but one, is very immaterial.

'This Iſland is full of palm and other trees, with ſandy beaches; and from the S. E. round to N. a large ſhoal of ſand. It lies N. and S. and is 10 or 12 leagues (34′ or 41′) in circuit: it is even with the water; and they found ſuch plenty of fiſh, that they caught them with their hands; and birds of different kinds, which they caught in the ſame manner: they found ſoundings, but ſo near ſhore, ſo much expoſed, and the ground ſo bad, that they durſt not anchor.

Torquemada,

Torquemada, in the relation of Quiros's voyage 1606, does not give the longitude of S. Bernardo; but as it was not seen on S. Bernardo's day, and as Quiros does not name S. Bernardo in the lift of his difcoveries, this is obviously the fame he fo named in his former voyage; and by this fituation his preceeding difcoveries are regulated.

Lat. & Long. from London. 10° 40′ S. 171° 28′ W.

The next Iflands to be mentioned were difcovered by the Dutch in 1722. The French relation fays, " Thefe Iflands are three in number, of a very agreeable profpect; they were found to be well provided with fruit-trees, all kinds of herbs, legumens, and plants. The inhabitants came on board with fifh, cocoa-nuts, plantains, and other excellent fruits, for which they received fome baubles and cutlery. Thefe Iflands are well peopled, for the fhores were covered with many thoufand men and women, the greateft part carried bows and arrows; one was taken for their chief, from the refpect fhewn him; he was in a canoe with a woman young and white, who fat at his

15° S. 173° 3′ W.

E   fide;

Geographical Description of

side; several vessels kept around with much eagerness, and served as guards. All they who inhabit these Islands are white, and not different from Europeans, but that some amongst them have their skins burnt by the heat of the sun. They appear lively and gay in their conversation, gentle and humane towards one another, and in their behaviour not the least appearance of savageness *

They

* The Dutch relation says, " 14th June, We " discovered two Islands which we could not approach " near enough to take a proper view thereof on ac- " count of the rough sea; but the inhabitants came " to take a view of us, and kept hovering about the " ships in a number of boats, of such neat and ex- " quisite workmanship, as is almost incredible that " any thing of the kind should have been found " among such uncivilized people; they were of so " artful a construction, the furniture so pretty, and " the form so neat, adorned with a number of the " most curious figures, that it is impossible for the " imagination to conceive any thing more elegant; " and really their carved image-work (which was " the greatest ornament of these boats) was so ex- " quisite, that I much doubt if there are many car- " vers in Europe capable of producing more curious " workmanship. The people in these fine boats " were armed with darts. They have their heads
" adorned

They had not their bodies painted as in the Iflands before difcovered, they were cloathed, from the middle downwards, with fringes, and with a kind of filk ftuff curioufly woven. Their heads were covered with hats, extreamly fine and very large, to fhade them from the heat of the fun ; around the neck they wore ftrings of odoriferous flowers. The Iflands every where prefented objects very agreeable : they were interfperfed with hills and vallies very pleafantly ; fome were 10, 15 to 20 leagues (40', 60' to 80') in circuit : they were named Bauman Ifles, from the Captain of the Tienhoven who firft faw them. It appeared each family had a diftinct jurifdiction : the country, as far as could be feen, was divided into partitions, as at Eafter Ifland. It was the moft

" adorned with green leaves, and their bodies
" cloathed with rufhes. This Ifland got the name
" of Bauman's Ifland, from a Captain of that name
" belonging to one of the fhips. It was very plea-
" fant and delightful to behold, fruitful and fur-
" rounded with trees, among which the palmeto
" fhewed itfelf. 15th June, Came in fight of an
" Ifland about 7 leagues (28') lying in 13° 41' S.
" We did not ftop here."

civilized

civilized nation the Dutch faw in the Iflands of the South Sea : All the coafts of thefe Iflands had good foundings, they anchored in 15 to 20 fathom *."

The next Ifland, difcovered by Quiros, which from its inhabitants was named Ifla-de Gente-hermofa (Ifland of Beautiful People) lies very nearly in a meridian with Bauman's Iflands.

In Mendana's voyage, ftanding Weftward from S. Bernardo, they had fome fhort and heavy fhowers of rain, and fuch fixed clouds, that they imagined there was land near them. In Quiros's voyage, after leaving S. Bernardo going Weftward, they had many birds about them, from whence they concluded they were near land. And,

* The French relation fays, " That leaving Bau-" man Iflands, and continuing their courfe to the " N.W. they next day faw two Iflands, one in " 11° S. very high, about 8 leagues (24′) in circuit. " The other appeared much lower. It was a red-" difh land with trees, but both were at too great a " diftance to be particularly defcribed."

On

" On 2d March 1606, Quiros in the morning early difcovered land to the Weftward. They lay-to till fun-rife, and then made fail for it. They fetched it on the North-fide; they faw fmoaks in the middle of the Ifland. The fmall fhip, being fent ahead, difcovered near the fhore amongft palms, a town of thatched houfes, from whence came out about 100 Indians, who were in effect cruel enemies, tho' they did not fhew it in their countenances and appearance, for they were the genteeleft, moft beautiful and whiteft people they found in the whole voyage. They have a vaft number of fmall piraguas, three or four Indians coming in each: they are extremely fleet made of one tree; they came in them along-fide of the fhips, making motions to fhew their courage, and brandifhing very large lances, which are the common arms they ufe. They were thrown from the fhips fome things, as well food as cloathing, to induce them by good offices to come aboard; but they, taking what was given them, rowed off: a young man came off in a narrow

E 3   piragua,

piragua, he had on his head a tuft made of the palm, and a kind of fhirt alfo of palm, but all red ; he came to the balcony of the Capitana, where fome ftood admiring his daringnefs, when he made a thruft, intending to kill one of them, getting off as faft as he could with his piragua.

A large squadron attempted to deftroy the Zabra, where fhe lay in 10 fathom, having leaped into the water, and come along-fide, they thought to have funk her; but, finding this impoffible, they got a long rope from the fhore, and making it faft to the prow of the Zabra, endeavoured to drag her afhore; perceiving that the Spaniards were preparing to cut it, they got a little off, and made the fame rope faft to the cable by which the Zabra rode; but the boats which were fent with 60 men to its affiftance, arriving, they fwam toward the fhore, fome being killed and others wounded. The Spaniards returned to the fhips which were at anchor a little farther off.

Next

Next day they fent 60 men, with the Zabra and boats, on purpofe to land to get wood and water: the Spaniards found it very difficult to land on account of the furf, and above 150 Indians came to the fhore, all with fhort lances, determined to revenge the injury they had fuffered; but the Spaniards firing on them from the boats, left fome dead amongft the rocks on the fhore, and put the reft to flight.

The Spaniards being all landed with difficulty, marched in regular order towards the town, where they found 10 or 12 Indians, all old men, moft of them had refinous fticks which they burnt as links, a fign amongft them of peace and friendfhip. The others having fled into the wood, where were their children and wives, near a large lagune which the fea made with flood-tide. Coming up to the Indians of the town, who waited for them, they found them with their lighted links in their hands, and fome of them with green boughs, which they gave to the Spaniards, humbling themfelves with

E 4   great

great marks of fear. Amongſt the others came one Indian handſome and of large ſtature, tho' old ; of him the Spaniards begged water, ſhewing him a piece of taffaty : he ſeemed much pleaſed, and went to conduct 14 or 15 Spaniards who followed him ; arriving near the lagune, having paſſed the town, they found a large brook, but of brackiſh water. Hither came an Indian with a cocoa-nut ſhell of freſh water ; and, on being aſked whence it was brought, replied, from the other ſide of the lagune ; ſome Spaniards were ſent with him to ſee where it was, the Indian ſhewing the way. Theſe men went to the gardens where all the Indians had retired, who ſeeing the Spaniards, came out to make peace, and alſo ſome women of a good diſpoſition and beauty, and ſome of them in extreme degree ; and altho' a barbarous people, born and bred in theſe remote parts, expoſed to the rigour of the ſun, of the air and cold (reaſon enough to be burnt up and black) they were exceſſively white, principally the women, who, were they cloathed, would

without

without doubt excel our Spanifh ladies, ac-
companying their gracefulnefs and beauty
with modefty and bafhfulnefs, they looked
with down-caft eyes, and very feldom, approaching to embrace our people with de-
monftration of love and peace according to
their cuftom. They go covered from the
waift downward, with white mats of palm,
fine and well worked, carrying others in the
manner of mantles, made of the fame palm
with which they cover their fhoulders.

The Spaniards came to one of the gardens,
where, guided by the Indians, they found a
fmall brook of frefh water; and, altho' it
formed a pool, it was fo fmall, that it was
impoffible to water the fhips with it.

One of the Spaniards being fent to give
this intelligence to the fhips, as he paffed by
the houfes of the Indians, he was attacked
by 10 or 12, who came out with miffile
darts with fharp burnt points, and large
clubs and wooden fwords. He could fcarce
defend himfelf, being wounded in the hand
and

and face: the reft of the Spaniards coming to his affiftance clofed with the Indians, of whom four or five were killed, and fome others wounded. Of thofe who were killed, fuch was the courage and fpirit of one, that it much difgraced the Spaniards, for naked and without arms, except a club in his hand, he defended himfelf againft more than twenty foldiers well armed, acting offen-fively, as if he had equal arms, and defend-ing himfelf a very long time, and making as it were a fort of his club, he did not let one of his enemies come near him, who enraged at the favage, ceafed not to attack him with their fwords, well covered by their targets, to which the valiant favage gave furious blows, and tho' they were fheltered under them, he did not fail to annoy them; but as the foldiers were many, and the Indian alone, he funk with fatigue tho' not with fear. The Spaniards advanced upon him, and fome of them gave him many wounds, yet not for this did the Indian, inflamed with rage, give over to attack our people, till fatigued, and fpent with lofs of blood,
he

he dropt dead, biting the earth in horrid agonies: leaving all the Spaniards full of admiration to behold his valour, and of regret to have taken that life, which he had so well defended againſt ſuch numbers.

The Spaniards went from thence to the gardens in queſt of food and people, but they were diſappointed, for all the Indians had fled, and of the hindmoſt, who were getting away as faſt as they could, were two old people, appearing to be man and wife, who being ſeen by the Spaniards they purſued them; the old man ſeeing it was impoſſible to eſcape thoſe who purſued, and concluding from what had paſſed, that they ſhould loſe their lives, was ſolicitous that his companion ſhould eſcape, and perſuaded her to fly into a little wood hard by; the Indian obeyed at her huſband's requeſt, and left him alone, till the Spaniards came up, when they ſeized him to carry him to the Armada, tho', on account of his great age, they thought he would be uſeleſs for their purpoſe, which was to carry him away that they might get

ſome

some information of the country; they were about leaving him when the old woman who had run away came out to them, fignifying that fhe would rather die with him than live alone, which alfo raifed great aftonifh-ment in the Spaniards; they left them to-gether and returned to the boats: the two old people, happy and grateful for their de-liverance, went to the town."

The Spaniards got off with great diffi-culty, one of the boats was overfet and the people faved by fwimming, they were much wounded in the feet by the fharp points of the fea eggs which lay on the fhore between the water and the rocks; thefe wounds took many days to cure.

As there was no harbour or water here, they determined to leave the Ifland; it lies N. and S. and is 6 leagues (21′) in circuit, it is named Ifla de Gente-hermofa (Ifland of Handfome People) in Torquemada; but Quiros's memorial calls it N° Sen* del Socorro.

Neither

Neither the latitude nor longitude of this Island is particularly mentioned, but it is probably rather under than above 10° S. for Quiros standing westward from thence for Santa Cruz in 10° 20′ S. made Taumaco in 10° S.

Lat. & Long. from London.

" Solitary, a small round Island, low and full of trees, was discovered by Mendana, 29th August 1595. It is about a league ($3\frac{1}{2}$′) in circumference, and quite surrounded with reefs and rocks above water. The small vessel anchored in 10 fathom, but the shore was full of great rocks, visible under water, as they had sometimes 10 fathom, and sometimes no ground 100."

10° 40′ S. 179° 50′ W.

As the future discoveries of Mendana, Quiros, and Schouten, are farther West than Tasman's Rout, they cannot be considered as immediately connected with the Continent; it is therefore proposed to recite the discoveries of Tasman from New Zeland or Staat's Land North-Eastward.

On

" On 13th December 1642, Tafman dif-covered a very high mountainous country 15 miles (60′) diftant, which is now called in the charts New Zeland, but Tafman named it Staat's Land.

18th. They anchored in a fine bay, lat.

40° 50′ S. where they were not long with-out feeing the favages, but their firft figns did not tend to infpire the Dutch with much confidence.

They found here abundance of inhabi-tants, they had very hoarfe voices, and were very large made people; they durft not ap-proach the fhips nearer than a ftones-throw. They were often obferved playing on a kind of trumpet, to which the Dutch anfwered with the inftruments aboard their veffels. The natives were in complexion between brown and yellow; their hair black, and almoft as long as the Jappanefe, and made up on the crown of their head, with a great thick white feather in the middle. Thefe people cover the fore-part of their bodies,

fome

fome with a piece of mat, others with a
cotton cloth; the reft were naked. Some
played on an inftrument, the found of which
refembled a trumpet.

On the 19th, thefe natives began to grow
a little bolder and more familiar, infomuch
that they at laft ventured on board the
Heemfkirk, in order to trade with the people
aboard, as foon as Tafman perceived it, being apprehenfive they might attempt to fur-
prize the fhip, he fent his boat with feven
men to put them on their guard. The boat's
crew being unarmed, were attacked by the
natives, who killed three, and forced the
other four to fwim for their lives, whence
he named the place *Murderer*'s Bay. The
fhip's company would have taken a fevere
revenge, if rough weather had not prevented
them.

From this bay he bore away Eaft, having
land all around. This country appeared
rich, fertile, and very well fituated; but as
the weather was very foul, and the wind

5   ftrong

ſtrong at Weſt; he found it very difficult to clear the land.

The 24th, the wind not permitting to continue the courſe to the North, as they were uncertain whether there was to be found any paſſage that way, and as the flood came in from the S. E. * it was concluded to be beſt to return into the bay, and ſeek ſome other way out.

But, on the 26th, the wind coming more favourable, Taſman continued his rout to the North, a little inclining to the Weſt.

On the 4th January 1643, he ſailed quite to the N. W. cape of this land, where he found the ſea rolling in from the N. E. whence it was concluded a paſſage was at laſt found. An Iſland, at a ſmall diſtance, they named the Iſland of Three Kings, be-cauſe the ſhips approached it on that day. They doubled the cape of it with intention

* If the flood comes from S. E. it would ſeem this land was not Continent but Iſlands.

to

to refresh, but approaching it, they observed
on the mountain 30 or 40 persons, who,
as far as could be discerned at that distance,
were men of very large size, and had each
of them a large club in his hand; they called
out in a strong rough voice, but the Dutch
could not understand any thing they said.
They observed these people walked at a
great rate, and that they took prodigious
large strides. The Dutch made the tour
of the Island, in doing which they saw but
very few inhabitants, nor did any of the
country appear to be cultivated. They found
indeed a fresh-water river, where they intended to get some water, but were prevented by an accident.

Tasman resolved to sail East as far as
177°, and then North to 17° South latitude,
and thence Westward to the Islands of Co-
cos and Horne, where he intended to refresh,
in case they found no opportunity of doing
it before; for the weather prevented their
setting foot on New Zeland.

Long. & Lat.
from London.
40° 50′ S.
169° 16′ E.

F 8th

Lat. & Long.
from London.
32° 25′ S.
169° 55′ E.

8th January, there was a high rolling fea from S. W.

29° 50′ S.
173° 2′ E.

12th, Had a rolling fea from S. E. and S. W.

22° 57′ S.
178° 10′ W.

19th, Tafman difcovered an Ifland about 2 or 3 leagues (8′ or 12′) in circuit, which feemed to be very high, fteep and barren: they were defirous of approaching it, but were prevented by S. E. and S. S. E. winds; they named it Pylftart Ifland, from the great number of that fort of birds they faw flying about it.

On the 20th, they had fight of two other Iflands. And

21° 20′ S.
176° 56′ W.

On the 21ft, they drew near to the coaft of the moft Northern Ifland, which was the higheft and largeft of the two; this they named Amfterdam, the other Middleburgh. Upon Amfterdam they found great plenty of hogs, fowls, and all forts of fruit, and other refrefhments. The natives did

not

not feem to have the ufe of arms, as nothing like them was feen in any of their hands. While upon this Ifland, the ufage the Dutch met with was fair and friendly, except that the natives would fteal a little. The current is not very confiderable at this place; it ebbs N. E. and flows S. W. The tide rifes full feven or eight feet; a S. W. moon makes high water. They wind blew conftantly S. E. or S. S. E. They took in no water, as it was not eafily come at.

Lat. & Long. from London.

On the 25th, After having had fight of feveral Iflands, they made one called Annamocha by the natives, but which the Dutch named Rotterdam. The natives refemble thofe of Amfterdam, were very good-natured, parting readily with what they had, and did not feem to be acquainted with the ufe of arms, but were given to thieving like thofe of Amfterdam. They watered here, and took in other refrefhments with all imaginable conveniency. They made the circuit of the whole Ifland, and found it well ftocked with cocoa-nut trees, very

20° 15′ S. 176° 15′ W.

regularly

regularly planted: they likewife faw abundance of gardens, extremely well laid out
in fquares, and plentifully ftocked with all
kinds of fruit-trees, planted in ftrait lines,
and the whole kept in fuch excellent order
that it was a pleafure to behold them, and
on all fides they afforded a fragrant and delightful fmell." After quitting this, they
had fight of feveral other Iflands. They
however ftood to the Northward, and in
17° 19′S. they difcovered a clufter of Iflands,
environed with rocks and fhoals: but thefe,
and the future incidents of Tafman's voyage, as without relation to the Continent,
are not to be mentioned in this place.

The cuts Valentyn has publifhed of Tafman's voyage compenfate, in fome meafure,
for the very brief relation of the journal,
which does not even mention the complexion of the natives of Amfterdam and
Rotterdam, and has omitted to defcribe the
embarkations, &c. of the Indians.

CONDUCT

CONDUCT of the DISCOVERERS in the Tracks they made choice of.

THE voyages previous to Mendana's expedition in 1595, are not known precifely enough to come under this examination. The object in Mendana's voyage feems to have been an eftablifhment at S. Chriftoval *, with the view to have profecuted from thence his difcoveries to the South. It was at this time conjectured, that the land extended from New Guinea almoft to the Streight of Magellan; and therefore forming an eftablifhment on one of the Iflands, was only confidered as a prelude to the reduction of the great Continent. As we have no circumftantial relation of Mendana's voyage in 1575, it is impoffible to determine what were his particular motives for making choice of S. Chriftoval for this previous eftablifhment: but we may form a conjecture why he did not forego

---

* An Ifland he had difcovered in 1575.

this

this object on difcovering the Marquefas,
which Iflands are defcribed to be in every
refpect well adapted for an eftablifhment.
It could not be a peremptorinefs in his in-
ftructions, for had they been exprefs to efta-
blifh S. Chriftoval only, he would not, in
difobedience to them, have fixed at the
Ifland Santa Cruz. The reafon appears to
be this ; as New Guinea approaches to the
Equator, it was conjectured the Continent
extended in a direct line from thence toward the Magellanick Strait ; and, on this
account, two places in the fame latitude,
were conceived to be very differently fituated
in relation to the Continent : hence the Marquefas were concluded to be much farther
diftant from the Continent, than S. Chriftoval or Santa Cruz, and therefore lefs proper
for the purpofes of the intended eftablifhment.

Mendana, from what remains of his fentiments, does not appear with much advantage as a difcoverer ; his vague ideas of the
fituation of the Iflands whereto he was

5   bound

bound are amazing, tho', on attentive obfervation in them, we fhall find the fource
of the ill fuccefs of this expedition; for
three or four days after leaving the Marquefas, he faid, "They fhould that day fee
"the land they fought," but faw none in
many days after. They left the Marquefas
5th Auguft, and on the 20th they made
S. Bernardo. Not finding the land, according to Mendana's prediction, much difcou-
raged the foldiers, who had been extravagant
of their water and provifions on hearing the
land was nigh, and by that began to feel the
inconveniencies to be expected from fuch in-
difcretion. "Irrefolution and defpair * be-
"gan to prevail, and few were undaunted,
"nor is it to be admired, for fuch under-
"takings require men inured to fufferings,
"and patient in them." This ill difpofition
was encreafed, when on the 29th they difcovered and left Solitary Ifland, continuing
their courfe to the Weftward: "Many
"people giving their fentiments: fome fay-
"ing they did not know where they were

* Fragment.

F 4   "going

" going, and other such reflections, which
" (as Quiros observes) could not fail of
" raising uneasinesses."

Here we find the source of all the disputes which afterwards arose, and terminated in the publick execution of some of
the principal officers : nothing is so requi-
site for the fortunate execution of such voyages, as a confidence in the knowledge of
the commander ; unless it be the general
opinion that he is better able to conduct
them than any other, endless discords must
arise, and nothing but ruin and destruction
can be expected to ensue.

Losing company of the Almiranta was
another cause of Mendana's ill success. Ac-
cidents of this kind are almost unavoidable
in a squadron ; but when they happen, dis-
concert measures so much, that they are
scarce ever surmounted. The apprehension
of the loss of their companions strikes a
damp into the spirits of the people, who
consider it as a prelude to their own ; and
                                    the

the natural difpofition of man to trace caufes, will generally fettle them in a fufpicion, at leaft, of their commander's conduct; for poft facto reafoning is very clear in its determination ; if every meafure be taken for a rejunction, other objects muft be given up; and if every idea of every man is not followed, it will be alledged as an objection to the commander. A thoufand motives recommend a fingle fhip for difcovery : tho' indeed as Mendana's expedition was rather to make an eftablifhment than on difcovery, there was a propriety in having feveral veffels, and nothing but the ignorance of what he was in queft of, can be given as the fource of their misfortunes.

Quiros, previous to his expedition in 1606, as is obvious from the purport of the memorials prefented to Don Louis de Velafco, had formed a conclufion that there was a Southern Continent. This Continent was the ultimate object of his voyage in 1606.

5

It

It was his intention, when he left Peru, to proceed to the Santa Cruz Iflands, where he knew there was good fhelter and refrefh-ments, and from thence to profecute the difcovery.

Arias fays, " Quiros's companions, parti-cularly the Admiral Louis Vaez, who ftrongly importuned him to that effect, were of opi-nion that they fhould have gone into 40° S. as it was very conformable to reafon that they fhould thus find the Continent they fought: Quiros for certain reafons refufed, and particularly becaufe he was apprehenfive of bad-weather, feeing the fun was declin-ing towards the equinoctial, but he found his refufal a very wrong ftep."

Perhaps Quiros's conduct, on examina-tion, will not appear fo faulty as he himfelf feems to have allowed; it is very natural to think any meafures better than thofe which have proved unfuccefsful.

Arias

Arias leaves us to guefs the other reafons for Quiros's conduct, that he mentions is a ftrong one. The danger of a high latitude at the Equinox is certainly unfavourable to difcovery, and the bad weather Quiros had in 28° S. fhews how much he had confidered the fubject. However it muft not be forgot that the feafons within the limits of the trade winds, are very different from what is common in higher latitudes. In thefe, fummer and winter regulate in good mea-fure the winds and weather; in the tropical regions fair weather attends the fettled trade or eafterly winds, foul weather the wefterly winds; except where a chain of mountains alters the general rule. In the fouthern lati-tudes, during their fummer-months, the wefterly winds prevail, and are accompanied by rains and bad weather, fo that perhaps Quiros, as the fummer was not over, would have had fair weather in 40° S. at the time he had the weather fo bad in 28° S.

If, as Arias mentions, Quiros was deftined for the Santa Cruz Iflands, that undoubtedly

was

was reason sufficient for him not immediately to change the purpose of the expedition. Perhaps his plan was the most eligible, for had the squadron proceeded directly to the Santa Cruz Islands and established themselves there, the expedition would not have proved abortive as it did, and the important discoveries they had in view would have been secured by a more certain, tho' less precipitate measure.

Perhaps Quiros was induced, by the solicitations of his companions, to deviate from his intended rout: his ill-luck in the Islands he discovered from 25° to 28° S. none whereof afforded him water or anchorage, obliged him to stand to the northward: altho' at Sagittaria in 17° 40′ S. he received intimation of large countries in his way, this Island could yield him no supplies, and this disappointment seems to have determined him to get immediately into the parallel of Santa Cruz.

This

This feems his moft reprehenfible ftep, for the intimation he received, at Sagittaria, of large countries, ought to have induced him to direct his courfe to the weftward, and nothing but the want he was in of water and provifions, can be urged as an excufe.

If there is any part of the Continent in a low latitude, he muft very foon have feen it, as Sagittaria is not above 20° to the eaft-ward of Tafman's Rout, and Le Maire's obfervation of having found fmooth water in this fituation, makes it probable that the land was not far diftant. However, thefe probabilities, from fubfequent difcoveries, are no imputation on Quiros, who could not be otherwife than ignorant of them.

Quiros feems alfo culpable in not pur-fuing the figns he had of the Continent in 26° S. the want of water appears alfo to have been the motive of his conduct in this inftance.

Quiros,

Quiros, having got the supplies he required of wood and water at Taumaco in
10° S. about 6° to the eaftward of Santa
Cruz, defifted from going to fettle at the
Santa Cruz Iflands, in confequence of the
intimation he received from the Cazique or
Chief of Taumaco, " that if they were in
queft of the great Continent it was much
more probable they would find it by going
to the South than to the Santa Cruz Iflands,
for that to the South were countries very fertile and populous and of great depth extending due South."

It was extreamly unfortunate for Quiros,
that none of the Iflands he difcovered, before Taumaco, could yield him the requifite
fhelter and fupplies : in that cafe, he would
undoubtedly have ftood to the fouthward,
nor can it be doubted, that this meafure
would have difcovered to him the *Great
Southern Continent*, or, as he emphatically
expreffes himfelf, *The Mother of fo many
Iflands*. Quiros, ftanding to the S.W. from
Taumaco, difcovered feveral Iflands ; and
                                        foon

foon after, in 15° 20′ S. a large country, which is evidently the Manicola, whereof he had intimation at Taumaco. He named it *Tierra Auftralia del Efpirito Santo* (the Southern Land of the Holy Ghoft) very naturally conjecturing it to be part of that Continent of which he was in purfuit, tho' by Tafman's Rout we are now affured it is not the Continent, but a very large Ifland, whofe eaftern exremity is hitherto undifcovered.

Quiros, being unluckily feparated from his conforts, directed his courfe for the Santa Cruz Iflands, which had been appointed a place of rendezvous, but, falling to leeward, he was conftrained to bear away for Mexico. In one of his memorials he alledges, that he was much impeded by ficknefs; fo that it is rather to be wondered he did *fo much*, than that he did not effect *more*. He feems to have conducted himfelf, in general, much more difcreetly than other voyagers; and, much to his honour, there is not the leaft femblance of a jealoufy of his Admiral,

who

who feems to have been very active and dif-
creet, if we except his foolifh punto of paffing the line drawn by the Indians at Vera
Cruz, as a fign to the Spaniards not to come
too near, whereby a fcuffle enfued, in which,
tho' the Indian chief was killed, the Spaniards fuffered moft, as all their difappoint-
ments arofe from the want of thofe provifions and refrefhments which the country
was very capable to have afforded them.

The rout of Le Maire was apparently
directed by fome hints he had of Quiros's
difcovery in 15° 20′ S. Being ignorant of
the longitude, they kept near the latitude
of 15° S. croffing the Pacifick Ocean in
that parallel. Had they continued their
courfe weftward, inftead of ftanding to the
northward, the day before they difcovered
Horne Ifland, a very fhort time muft have
brought them to the country which Quiros
had difcovered, and to which he gave the
name of Auftralia del Spirito Sancto. Le
Maire fays he meant to go 50 leagues (200′
or 3° 20′) farther, before he changed his
courfe,

courſe, but the ſailors and the council not conſenting, he could not execute this purpoſe. He then adviſed to ſteer N. W. towards the point of New-Guinea, hoping, by this means, both parties would be ſatis-fied, and that in doing ſo he could not fail to find the Iſlands which are to the North of the bay St. Philip and St. Jago in 13° S.

" The pilot replied, that by this courſe, inſtead of the point, they would get to the middle of New-Guinea, and, in caſe of not finding a paſſage to the South of it, which was very hazardous and uncertain, that then the ſhip and goods would be loſt, and every one periſh, as it was impoſſible to return to the Eaſt, on account of the con-ſtant eaſterly winds, which blow in theſe parts ; that beſides they were badly provided with proviſions, and that there was no ap-pearance of any means of recruiting them ; he therefore propoſed to ſail to the northward, at leaſt to be aſſured of falling in to the North of New-Guinea, and thence to proceed on to the Moluccas. It was thereupon con-

G cluded

cluded by the council *to stand North, not to
fall to the South of New-Guinea in incertainty,
but on the North to find an assured track.*"

Nothing can more expose Schouten's ignorance and ill conduct than the resolution
of this council, nor can any thing do greater
honour to Le Maire's ability than the oppo-
sition he made to this determination : had
they been in possession of Quiros's relation,
and of Torres's, there could not have remained a doubt that there was a passage to
the South of New-Guinea : but, even ignorant as they were, Schouten's argument was
very weak, for if there was no passage they
must have been brought to the country they
sought : indeed he seems to have thought all
Quiros's discoveries *imaginary*, which is the
natural conclusion of a little ignorant mind.

However, this voyage, being obviously
directed to the land Quiros had discovered
in 15° 20′ S. leaves no room for animad-
version, as they crossed the Pacifick Ocean
in this latitude, and when they despaired of
finding

finding *it*, made their way to the northward till they got into the parallel of New-Guinea.

Le Maire, with a sneer, says, when the Patron* found the cove at Horne Island, " He said, here was the *true* Terra Austra-" lis, seeing that here was found a river of " fresh water, many hogs seen ashore, and " plenty of other things; he even proposed " to stay five weeks there."

Le Maire's opinion of Hope and Horne Islands was, that they were the same named Solomon Islands, " Certainly (says he) they " correspond well to Quiros's description, " and no doubt the Terra Australis was very " near." His conjecture about the Solomon Islands is evidently erroneous, but it was necessary to take notice of it, as he gives a vocabulary of the language of Horne Island under that name.

W E have not sufficient ground to judge what was the precise object of Tasman's voy-

* Schouten.

age;

age; that of examining if New - Holland and New-Guinea were parts of the Southern Continent, seems to have been Tasman's chief intention; and this he determined in the negative. It remains still a question if Staat's Land or New-Zeland be part of that Continent, or only Islands, tho' it is most probably the former.

Various are the reports of the intention of Roggewein's voyage; the author of the French relation pretends Roggewein's father had, in 1669, delivered a memorial to the Dutch West-India Company, with a plan for discovering the southern regions, which was so well received, that the Company ordered three ships to be equipp'd, but the disturbances which then arose between Spain and the United Provinces, prevented the voyage from being undertaken. Old Roggewein at his death, exhorted his son not to lose sight of a matter so important, and in consequence of his application, tho' long delayed, this expedition was fitted out for the discovery of the southern lands. Others
                                                    pretend

pretend to have been well informed that this was lefs the object in purfuit than the examination of certain Iflands, named Golden Iflands, in 56° S.

After Roggewein left Juan Fernandes, he feems to have directed his courfe for the land feen by Davis, which he expected to find farther to the eaftward than that land is defcribed to be, fo that when he faw it, he thought it a new difcovery.

It appears from the track in the Dutch chart *, that, foon after leaving Eafter Ifland, they ftood to the N. W. and prefently croffed Quiros's track, fo that it was impoffible for them to have made any material difcovery; their track afterwards was fo nearly the fame as Schouten's, that it admitted of fcarce any thing new, except the Bauman Iflands near the meridian of Ifla de Gente-hermofa (Ifland of Beautiful People)

---

* I have examined almoft every diftance mentioned in the Dutch relation, and find thofe in the chart exactly confonant.

inhabited

inhabited by a civilized white people. In this neighbourhood there is great probability the point of the Continent approaches nearest the equator, and the favourable description given of the inhabitants of Bauman Islands, seems to indicate, that the natives of that country adjoining are very civilized.

After leaving these Islands, Roggewein passed to the northward of Taumaco, Santa Cruz, &c. and we have no account in the Dutch relation of their having seen any land, till they saw New-Britain, to which the chart also gives the name of New-Zeland. This chart describes their track to have been on the South of Onthong Java, which explains a circumstance related in the French; it says, " they discovered two very " large Islands, one whereof they named " Tienhoven, the other Groningue, the " former they coasted a whole day without " finding an end to it; it was of a mean " height, and appeared at a distance very " pleasant, of a fine verdure, and furnished " with trees." This Island appears to be what Mendana called S. Chriftoval in 1575. Le Maire alfo mentions it the night before he faw Onthong Java.

Roggewein's voyage would appear to have been wonderfully ill conducted, if we had not an intimation, that commercial views precipitated his meafures, for the figns of land, feeing teal, &c. for 12° to the eaft-ward of Eafter Ifland, pointed out very ob-vioufly the vicinity of the Continent, and muft have inflamed the purfuit of every real *difcoverer.*

Inveſtigation of what may be far-
ther expected in the SOUTH-SEA.

IN this diſquiſition, it is propoſed to inveſ-
tigate what may be farther expected in
the South Pacifick Ocean, as well from the
analogy of nature, as from the deduction of
paſt diſcoveries.

In the latter part of the 15th, during the
16th, and beginning of the 17th centuries,
a ſpirit of enterprize, inflamed perhaps by
avarice and enthuſiaſm, laid open the Eaſt-
Indies, America, and other remote regions
of the globe : this ſpirit of enterprize ceaſed
to actuate, at leaſt in the ſame channel, before the compleat examination of the world
was effected : hence the ſouthern regions remain ſtill indeterminate, and we continue
ignorant, ſo far as to abſolute experience,
whether the ſouthern hemiſphere be an im-
menſe maſs of water, or whether it contains
another

another continent, and countries worthy of
our fearch.

But, altho' the remote parts of the fouthern
hemifphere remain undifcovered, we have
traces from antient times, warranted by latter
experience, of rich and valuable countries
in it; no fubject can be more interefting, to
a commercial ftate, than the difcovery of
new countries and people, to invigorate the
hand of induftry, by opening new vents for
manufactures, and by introducing, from
new quarters, the comforts and convenien-
cies of life.

It has been commonly alledged, and perhaps not without good reafon, from a confideration of the weight of land to water,
that a Continent is wanting on the South of
the Equator, to counterpoize the land on
the North, and to maintain the equilibrium
necefifary for the earth's motion. On a view
of the two hemifpheres this will appear obvious: and what ftrengthens the opinion is,
that from the Equator to the Tropick, the
                                        proportion

proportion of land is nearly the fame in North and South latitude; the fpace of water being in both nearly double to the land. Tho' beyond the Tropick the proportion of land is very fmall to what is fuppofed fea.

The annexed Table will elucidate the comparative proportion, in fquare degrees, of land to water in the two hemifpheres, as well within the Tropicks as without, tho' it is not extended to the Poles, even of the northern polar regions, very little being known.

	North Lat.		South Lat.	
	Land.	Water.	Land.	Water.
0 to 10°	1100	2500	1200	2400
10 to 20°	950	2650	950	2650
20 to 23°	420	660	270	810
	2470	5810	2420	5860

The excefs of land in North latitude is very inconfiderable, being only 50 fquare degrees. This will probably be made up in in the Southern Lands and Iflands not yet difcovered.

	North Lat.		South Lat.	
	Land.	Water.	Land.	Water.
23 to 30°	980	1540	560	1960
30 to 40°	1700	1900	400	3200
40 to 50°	2200	1400	100	3500
	4880	4840	1060	8660

From the Tropick to 50° North latitude, the proportion of land and water is nearly equal ; but in South latitude, the land, hitherto known, is not $\frac{1}{8}$ of the fpace fuppofed to be water. This is a ftrong prefumption, that there are in the fouthern hemifphere, hitherto totally undifcovered, valuable and extenfive countries, in that climate beft adapted for the conveniency of man, and where, in the northern hemifphere, we find the beft peopled countries.

50 to Polar Circle	4155	1740	100	5660

So

So little is known here in the South Hemifphere, that there is fcarce room for a comparifon, and as the climate to the South in thofe latitudes, is probably too fevere for fuch countries to be of much value, they do not come within the object of the prefent difquifition.

What has been faid will naturally induce conviction, that from the Tropick to 50° South latitude there are extenfive countries; and, from a view of the globe, it will as naturally occur, that the moft probable fituations, in which thofe lands may be expected to approach neareft the Equator, are not where the American and African Continents project fartheft into the fouthern hemifphere; but in the intermediate fpaces between the Cape of Good Hope and America, and to the weftward of the laft, between it and Papua; the one oppofite to the Atlantick, the other to the North Pacifick Ocean. And as the tracks of Halley and Bouvet confine the former, fo that it cannot exceed 180 fquare degrees of land, there

is

is a farther prefumption of the vaft extent
of the Continent to the weftward of America.

From the Tropick to 50° N. the
    fquare degrees of land are - - 4880
In S. latitude at prefent known - - 1060
                                    ————
                                    3820
The track between Halley's and
    Bouvet's Routs - - - - - 180
                                    ————
                    Remains 3640

So much being wanting for the counterpoize between the Tropick and 50° S.
which muft lie either in the Pacifick Ocean
or to the eaftward of Africa ; Tafman's voyage proves, that if there be any land between thefe parallels to the eaftward of the
Cape of Good Hope, it can be but a fmall
proportion, and therefore the greateft part
muft lie to the weftward of America. The
breadth of the Pacifick Ocean from America to New-Zeland is in longitude about
120°, or perhaps fcarce fo much. The
                                    whole

whole space, containing only 3240 square degrees, falls short of the wanted counterpoize 3640 by 400 square degrees; this is as much as can be supposed to lie to the S.W. of New-Zeland, from thence to the latitude of 50° S. The voyages from Magellanica cut off about 270° on the East of this space of 3240 square degrees, Roggewein's track about 120, Quiros's track about 80, and Tasman's track to the N. E. of New-Zeland about 100 square degrees, in the whole 570, taken from 3240, there remains 2670 square degrees, which the possible tract of land in the South Pacifick Ocean cannot exceed, and the deficiency 570 must be found to the westward of New-Zealand, from Van Diemen's land towards Manicola ; and as there does not appear room for more land in that space than 570. The space unknown in the Pacifick Ocean, from the Tropick to 50° S. must be nearly all land.

It does not indeed follow that the whole counterpoize of land wanting in the southern

hemis-

hemifphere, fhould be found from the Tropick to 50° South latitude. For as the only natural divifion of the earth, is that of the antients into zones, if the counterpoize between the Tropick and Polar Circle be equal, it is not abfolutely required that the proportion between any other two intermediate parallels fhould be the fame in the two hemifpheres. However, as in the North from the Tropick to 50°, the proportion of land and water is nearly equal, we are led to an analogous conclufion that in the fouthern hemifphere it cannot be very much different, and altho' an inconfiderable deficiency, within thefe parallels, may be made up by an excefs towards the Antartick Circle, yet, as beyond the latitude of 50° North to the Polar Circle, the proportion of land to water encreafes fo as to be nearly three to one, we cannot, on that account, fuppofe any great excefs of land in the fouthern hemifphere beyond 50°, as well as becaufe a fquare degree in the lower latitudes occupies a much greater fpace on the

surface

surface of the globe, than a square degree nearer the Pole.

Having shewn that there is a seeming necessity for a Southern Continent to maintain a conformity in the two hemispheres, it rests to shew, from the nature of the winds in the South Pacifick Ocean, that there must be a Continent on the South.

The tropical regions in wide oceans have a constant easterly wind; but where there are extensive chains of land, these winds not only become in general less steady, but are interrupted, during some months of the year, by a westerly wind.

In North latitude, when the sun is to the northward of the Equator, the westerly winds prevail; at this time the winds are easterly in South latitude. When the sun gets to the South of the Equator, the westerly winds succeed in South latitude, and the easterly in North: as the winds in North latitude

latitude blow from S.W. fo in South latitude
do they blow from N.W. altering their direction ftill more northerly in fome places :
and as in the eaftern part of the China feas,
and in that part of the North Pacifick
Ocean on the Eaft of the Philipinas, it
often happens that, during the fummer-
months, the winds blow from S. S. E. to
E. S. E. inftead of S. W. So it will probably be found in the South Pacifick Ocean,
that the winds blow often from N. N. E.
and E. N. E. inftead of N. W. this devia-
tion is probably owing to the vicinity of the
fettled trade.

The wefterly winds are generally attended
both in North and South latitude, with
fqually and rainy weather. The eafterly
wind, on the contrary, brings with it fair
weather, except where a chain of mountains alters the general rule.

If there is no Continent, or extenfive
range of land in the South Pacifick Ocean,
there can be no variability of wind, but a

H   conftant

conftant S. E. and E. S. E. trade wind muft prevail the whole year. If this trade wind is not conftant, there muft undoubtedly be land.

Without infifting on the information we derive from Ulloa, that the Spaniards at fome diftance from the Peruvian fhore find S. W. winds, we fhall confine the difcuffion of this point to the teftimony of the voyages acrofs the Pacifick Ocean.

In the beginning of April the Dutch were driven off by a wefterly wind from Eafter Ifland.

About the middle of May, near Pernitious Iflands, the wind began to veer from S. E. to S. W.

10th April, the Dutch, when they difcovered Dog Ifland, had the wind at N. and the night after it blew very hard, with much rain.

In January, Quiros, in the courfe from Lima to La Encarnacion, had fometimes variable winds.

Le

Le Maire, two or three days after leaving Fly Ifland, in the middle of April, had the wind at N.

We have few intimations of the winds in Quiros's voyage; but the 14th February they feem to have had the wind northerly as they faw La Fugitiva bearing N.E. which, being much to leeward of it, they could not reach.

However, altho' there are in the voyages thro' the Pacifick Ocean, fo few inftances related of the winds, yet what are above recited will be fufficient to form an idea that there muft be land to change the direction of the wind. We have only to add on this head, from the author of *Chronica de la Provincia de S. Gregorio de las Philipinas,* a quotation he introduces from Quiros, fpeaking of appointing one of the galleons to Peru from Manila " por el camino, &c. For the " rout and voyage is I know much eafier and " fhorter than from Manila to New-Spain,"

which

which can only be if there are wefterly winds in the South Pacifick Ocean.

Having thus far confidered the philofophical reafons to expeɛt valuable and extenfive regions in the South Pacifick Ocean, it remains to examine the evidence to that effeɛt from paft difcoveries.

This tafk is confined to very few circumftances, for it is not in view to defcribe all the Iflands, and the arguments which may be drawn from the inhabitants of thefe Iflands, to prefume they are derived from, or have an intercourfe with, a Continent to the South.   It is meant to confine the confideration to fuch incidents as feem to relate in faɛt to the Continent, or to what appears to be very near it, and to elucidate the expeɛtations which may be from thence formed.

In the firft place muft be mentiòned the difcovery of Juan Fernandes, who in the paffage from Lima to Chili, having ftood to the weftward a certain diftance for the
                                        advantage

advantage of a fair wind, fteered South till he difcovered land, which he fuppofed to be the Southern Continent, as he faw on the coaft the mouths of very large rivers, from whence, and from what the natives intimated, he formed his conclufion. The country was very fertile and agreeable, and appeared much better and richer than Peru. It was inhabited by white people, of our ftature, very well difpofed, and cloathed with very fine cloths.

Altho' this appears to have been the firft difcovery of the Continent, there feems good reafon to think the Continent has been feen feveral times fince.

1599. By Theodore Gerrards, one of the firft Dutch who attempted to voyage into the South-Sea, who, after paffing the Streight of Magellan, being carried by tempefts into 64° South, in that height the country was mountainous and covered with fnow, looking like Norway, and feemed to

extend

extend towards the Islands of Salomon, that is to the North-westward.

1624. It is also said the Orange, one of the Nassau fleet, saw this Continent twice, in the passage from Cape Horne to Juan Fernandes, once in 50° South, and again in the latitude of 41° South.

Schouten and Le Maire had also signs of land near this situation, so that it cannot be doubted from so many concurrent testimonies, that the Southern Continent has been already discovered on the East-side. It appears more than probable, that Tasman's discovery, which he named Staat's Land, but which is in the maps called New-Zeland, is the western coast of this Continent. So that it appears this Continent in the latitude of 40° extends about 100° of longitude, which in this latitude is 4596′, a greater extent than the whole civilized part of Asia, from Turky eastward to the extremity of China.

5   The

The North coaſt of this vaſt Continent appears to be hitherto undiſcovered; for altho' Roggewein for a ſpace of 12° in longitude, in the latitude of 28° South, had ſigns of land, as teal and other land birds, &c. and Quiros alſo ſigns of the Continent farther to the weſtward in 26° South. We have no relation of any one having ſeen it.

Altho' the ſigns of land ſeen by Roggewein, previous to the diſcovery of Eaſter Iſland, denote the vicinity of the Continent, it is from his deſcription of that Iſland we are enabled to form ſome idea of the Continent adjoining: no voyage hitherto performed, points out ſo ſtrongly the original of the Peruvian manners and religion. That country from whence Mango Capac introduced arts, laws, manufacture, and all the comforts of civilized life, cannot fail of amply rewarding the fortunate people who ſhall beſtow letters inſtead of quippos, and iron in place of more awkward ſubſtitutes.

THE END.